A Little Bit One O'clock

Living with a Balinese Family

William Ingram

Ersania Books

Ersania Books
A Division of CV Rumah Roda
Jalan Kajeng #24, Ubud, Bali 80571, Indonesia

First printing 1998
Second printing 2002
Printed in Jakarta, Indonesia

Perpustakaan Nasional RI : Katalog Dalam Terbitan (KDT)
Ingram, William
   A Little Bit One O'clock : Living with a Balinese Family/ William Ingram. -- Denpasar : Ersania, 1997
   ... hlm. ; ... cm.

ISBN 979-95322-0-5

1. Bali -- Deskripsi. I. Judul

915. 985

Cover design by Saritaksu, Bali
Cover photograph by Jean Howe

To Jean

Contents

List of Illustrations

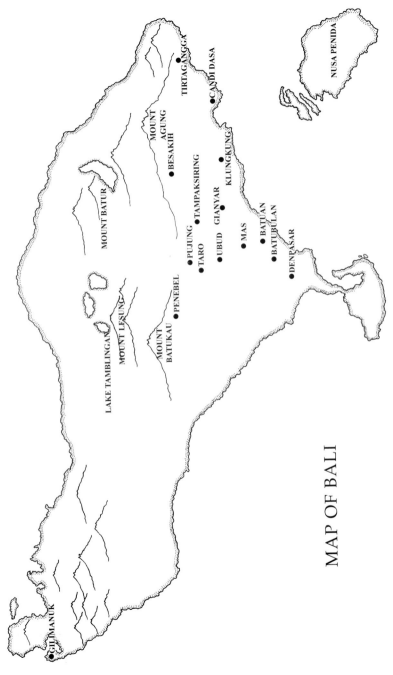

MAP OF BALI

NUSA PENIDA

TIRTAGANGGA

CANDI DASA

MOUNT AGUNG

BESAKIH

TAMPAKSIRING

KLUNGKUNG

GIANYAR

MOUNT BATUR

PUJUNG

TARO

UBUD

MAS

BATUAN

BATUBULAN

DENPASAR

PENEBEL

LAKE TAMBLINGAN

MOUNT LESUNG

MOUNT BATUKAU

GILIMANUK

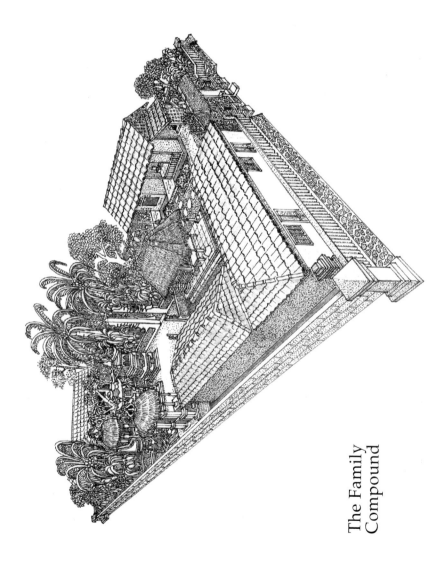

The Family
Compound

Family Tree

showing the principle characters in this book

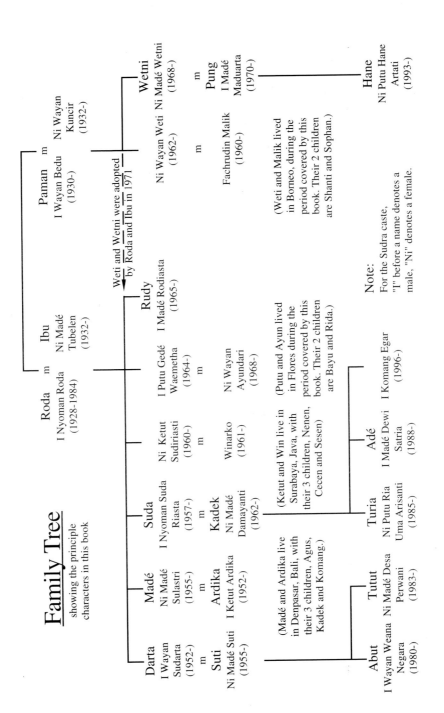

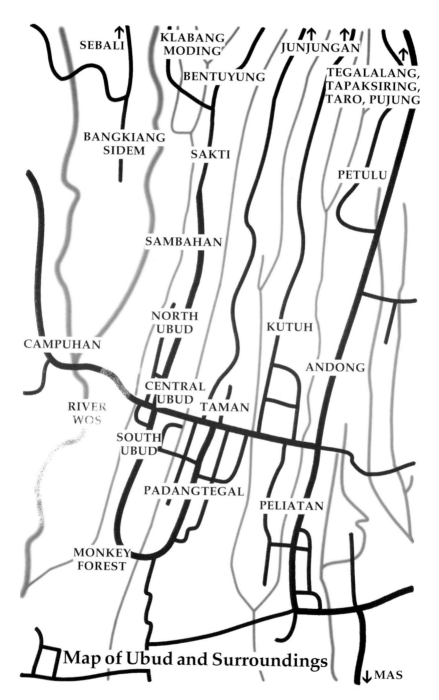

Map of Ubud and Surroundings

Author's Note

I have used the real names of all the major Balinese characters portrayed in this book. I wished to change their names to protect their privacy, but they all, without exception, asked me not to take their real names away from them. I have, therefore, endeavored to be obscure about the locations of their homes or villages.

The guidebook I refer to throughout our travels in Java is Lonely Planet's *Indonesia: a travel survival kit* by Robert Storey et al. Other sources worthy of note are *Island of Bali* by Miguel Covarrubias, *Bali: Sekala & Niskala, Volumes I & II*, by Fred B. Eiseman, Jr., *Dancing Shadows of Bali* by Angela Hobart, and *Ramayana* and *Mahabharata* by C. Rajagopalachari.

The United States dollar was worth 2,100 rupiah during 1993, when most of the events in this book took place.

CHAPTER 1

A Day in Bali

I awoke to the sound of roosters. There were hundreds of them. The nearest was right beside my room on the waist-high compound wall. Others scrabbled and crowed in a neighboring bamboo grove. The calls from across the whole village blended into a constant wailing.

A pale, pre-dawn light defined my room's pair of narrow, unglazed windows. Through these came the dry aroma of a coconut husk fire being kindled in the lean-to kitchen just inside the front gate. A change in the breeze brought the smell of a neighbor's pigs. Outside the door I heard someone moving around the courtyard sweeping away the lemon-white blooms that had fallen overnight from the frangipani tree. In the distance, from the community hall near the lotus pond, the village's wooden bell was sounding, slowly at first, then faster and faster. The bell was the heartbeat of the community. Its music called the people of North Ubud to the social or religious duties of the day. It called me to get up.

Sitting on the porch's edge, I watched the changing colors. The sun was low in the eastern sky and its light gilded the tops of the coconut trees. Looking down the garden path past the walled courtyard of the family temple, the kitchen and the open pavilion where visitors were received, I could see right through to the roofed front gate, forty yards away. I watched the family going about its early business.

Darta sat on the kitchen step in his underwear, drinking coffee. He was a rotund man in his late thirties. With him was his handsome younger brother Suda who wore a sarong and a T-shirt, and had a hatchet in a holster at his hip. For the previous three mornings Suda had been busy helping cut bamboo in preparation for a neighbor's cremation. For work, he ran the family's Cheap and Cheerful Café on the next street. Darta was responsible for the compound's four tourist rooms. He and his brother were close. From where I sat I couldn't hear what they were talking about, but I knew Darta was telling tales. He gesticulated wildly and Suda laughed. Just watching them made me happy.

Entering this little scene from stage-right came their mother, Ibu. She was in her late fifties. Her hair was long and gray and tied up in a bun. She wore an old batik sarong and a big white bra. In her arms she carried Suda's one-year-old son. She put him down on the kitchen floor and he began climbing his father.

It was just after seven o'clock on a November day in 1989. School had already started for the household's other children, and for Darta's school teacher wife, Suti. Suda's wife, Kadek, was just leaving. She worked in the offices of the island's water company. She wore a smart brown uniform and waved to her husband and son as she headed for the front gate.

Within the yard of the family temple, I could hear Pung singing to himself as he swept. Though not a family member by birth, he had become part of the clan by dint of long association. In 1985, his elder brother had been working with Kadek at the water company. "My little brother is very smart. He should have the opportunity to finish school," Wayan had said. Pung then came from their remote village to help at the café and began to work his way through high school, which he attended in the afternoons.

When the wooden bell sounded once more, Suda got up to leave. On his way out he stopped to bang on the bedroom door of his youngest brother, Rudy, who was to be Darta's substitute at the morning's community work. At the gate, Suda stopped to let his teenage sister enter. Wetni came in with a full load of laundry in a basket on her head. Minutes later, she left again, this time with an empty bucket for carrying water. She was headed for the river in the wooded canyon across the narrow tree-lined street. I heard laughter coming up from the canyon and could picture both the spring where she would collect water and the rock pools where other women washed.

I let out a deep sigh. Bali had overwhelmed me all over again, just as it had done every morning for the past two months. The family treated me as an honored guest and I was being reshaped by their tenderness. I often felt so raw that the view from the porch was all I could manage. It was a small window on a different world and the size of the frame made the impressions manageable.

As a long-term guest I was granted ready access to the dramas of the compound, but I was also somewhat separate. I watched the family moving like actors across a stage, left to right into the kitchen, right to left onto the pavilion. Then Ibu glanced my way. She waved and nodded, put her hand to her mouth and pronounced, *"Makan."* I nodded briefly, then repeated the word to the space where she had just been standing, tasting the strangeness of the two syllables at the back of my tongue.

Opening my notebook, I wrote the date by the left hand margin and immediately beneath it the word *makan*. Halfway across the page I wrote eat. The word was already part of my limited vocabulary, but I wrote it anyway. Its presence there in black and white was an affirmation of progress, a tether-peg for my cow-eyes. "You are making progress here," I told myself. "Sit and learn. Don't go galloping off over that hill, the grass won't be any greener. Sit tight—at least until after breakfast." My mind wandered all the same, my serenity blown to hell by the compulsion to visit a temple ceremony that had just begun in Bangli. "When was the last time you left this compound?" I chastised myself. "You haven't been on a tour for days! If you're not careful your camera's going to atrophy! Look at you! You can't even be a successful tourist!"

I heard Ibu call Pung away from his sweeping. A few moments later he came sauntering up the path with his brilliant teeth bared in a cocky school-boy grin, his T-shirt perfectly pressed, his jeans sharply creased, a fruit salad and a banana pancake on a tray held above his shoulder. He was followed by my host, Darta.

Rare indeed is the man who owns an ill-fitting sarong. There is so little to it. A simple rectangle of cloth, you just tie it on. Even so, Darta always made his look a little bit disheveled. He sat before me on the edge of the porch, his feet respectfully on a lower step while his stomach somewhat disrespectfully rolled over the tie of his sarong. This is how the day's informal language and culture lesson began.

"Ya, when I was a child we used to keep pigs back here. The pigs brought us money and food for ceremonies. Tourists are just the same."

"Thanks a lot, Darta." I mocked offense.

Darta laughed. I tried to keep a straight face, but couldn't.

"No, really," Darta continued. "Tourists are much more interesting than pigs. We're much better off than we used to be. And the conversation's better, too."

Darta liked to tease, but was always careful not to offend. Breakfast was always less sweet without his company and I awaited his morning visit as much as I looked forward to his mother's delicious food.

By eleven o'clock Darta was sitting next to me with both feet on the porch. The columns of my notebook were lost beneath my spider-like scrawls. That day's words were circled at the center of the layered web. As always, the lesson took off on unexpected tangents, which led neatly into lunch.

Darta often invited me to eat with him. We sat on the kitchen floor and ate with our hands, our plates piled with rice and various spicy vegetable condiments. After a nap, and once the heat of the day began to wane, I would take a walk up through the rice fields at the end of the street. The rice was newly planted. I loved the brightness of the young green shoots and the blue of the sky reflected in the flooded fields. The sound of running water was enchanting, as were the people I met along the way. The path was often in the shade of tall coconut trees and crossed two streams before making a slow, counter-clockwise circle which re-entered the village on its main road. I passed a dozen tourist shops and restaurants and, at the crossroads in the center of town, I turned north and walked the few hundred yards passed a huge banyan tree to the family café. My afternoon walks were slow and often circuitous, but always ended up at the café to collect my mail.

My girlfriend, Jean, wrote to me daily. By the time I'd read her letter a half-dozen times and written a reply, the late afternoon light had already begun its ocher descent toward night. For a few moments I became agitated. I'd lost another chance to visit Bangli. But I knew this was a passing fit and turned my thoughts toward dinner and the laughter of the family.

Every night, once the compound was quiet, I sat on my porch steps watching the night sky. I listened to the crickets and the breeze moving through the trees. My heart was so full I thought it might be breaking.

CHAPTER 2

Java, Anyone?

Jean and I had met in Tokyo at the end of 1988. We had both been teaching English. I was fresh out of college. Jean was fresh from two years living with Darta and his family in Ubud. She was blonde and as bright as the tropical sun. She always wore the scent of coconuts. Whenever she entered the room I thought of long walks on remote South Seas beaches. We were together for six months before she returned to Indonesia. Tokyo was desolate without her. After four months on my own, I followed her to Bali. We were together again for another two months before her money ran out and she left for Japan once more. She left me her family and her porch, and encouraged me to explore the island and its culture.

I had never intended to go so far. With a degree in mathematics I had planned to join the corporate world after my travels. But after a year in Japan and four months in Bali, I came to the realization that there was no going back to the conventional life I had lived before. An extended leave of absence had become a new way of life. I had seen too much, both of the nodding heads and vacant stares of exhausted commuters on the Tokyo subways, and of the lively light that shines from a pair of Balinese eyes. The former presented an uncomfortable mirror of my outward self. The latter offered a tantalizing glimpse of an inner world I felt compelled to explore.

I stayed on my own at Darta's for three months. My Indonesian improved rapidly. I would have stayed longer, but I missed Jean, and I was broke. Back in Japan, Jean and I moved in together and I went back to teaching. We spent three more years in Tokyo and our relationship continued to flourish. We took a month each year to visit Bali, and the sense of community we discovered with Darta and his family led us deeper into our commitment to one another. In September, 1992, we married. As our understanding of Bali deepened, so did our disillusionment with life in one of the world's largest cities. We longed for a simpler way of life, and left Japan at the start of April, 1993. Although we were not sure exactly where we were going, Bali was the obvious first stop.

Actually, our first stop was in Java.

We arrived in Jakarta after an eight-hour flight from Tokyo and spent a hot, stifling night at a cheap backpackers' guest-house in the heart of the city. Arising before dawn, we walked to a nearby train station and bought tickets to Semerang, a port on the north coast of central Java. This was where we were to meet the family.

We had written Darta a letter saying we were coming to Bali and mentioned our plans for a two-week exploration of Java. Darta's reply said he had decided to hire a car, take the family on its first-ever holiday, and come to see Java with us. We knew that spontaneity would be their holiday's guiding principle and that their itinerary would be in a constant state of flux. We might not see everything we had planned to, but we were sure to have fun.

We boarded our train at first light for a seven-hour ride, and pulled into Semerang station twelve hours later, in the middle of a thunderstorm. There were lightning strikes all around the horizon. The rumbles directly overhead were apocalyptic.

With guidebook in hand we took our bearings and set out for a nearby hotel. After a ten-minute walk we came to an intersection where there were two more roads in reality than there were on the map. Making a best guess, we soon became hopelessly lost. It took a further twenty minutes of scurrying through heavily pouring rain to travel the one block to the hotel.

The two-story Hotel Oewa-Asia stood back from the road in

the middle of what once might have been a garden, but was now a parking lot. We were shown only three rooms. The hotel was almost full. Most of the guests were Javanese: men with clean shirts, creased trousers and fist-fulls of gold rings, and women draped from head to foot in black. We were the only foreigners.

We chose the last available room with its own shower. The room boy took about ten seconds to show us around. "Very simple," he said. He wasn't kidding. The room was large and empty except for a double bed cleanly divided by a slender "Dutch wife" bolster.

With the room boy gone I stripped and jumped into the shower. "I've been looking forward to this all day!" I whooped to Jean. The shower ran brown, gurgled and then ran dry. Only my feet were wet. We grumbled for a while about the extra money we'd paid for the shower, then noticed that the rain had stopped and quickly set out for dinner.

"The Toko Oen is not to be missed," said the guidebook. We should have known better, but had no other way of choosing a place to eat. "It has good food and a great selection of ice creams." I was practically drooling at the prospect of something other than fried rice. We were less than a hundred yards from the hotel when it started to pour again.

A general store we were running past was still open. "Umbrellas!" said Jean, and we ducked in. As we paid for our goods one of the five women shop assistants said, "You must still have a long way to go tonight. You're already soaking wet, and now you buy an umbrella."

"We're looking for a restaurant called Toko Oen," I said.

They all laughed hysterically. They kept pointing towards the street and laughing. "You foreigners are so funny!" one of them gasped. We turned towards the street again, looking for the source of their hilarity, and there, right before us, across the street, was Toko Oen.

With its wicker chairs and white tablecloths, the establishment put on the airs of a colonial watering hole, but it wasn't the Raffles

Hotel by any stretch of the imagination. A pair of smart, if elderly, uniformed waiters sat at the end of the long bar, but it was a boy in jeans who came to serve us. The menu stretched to three pages, of which one-third dealt solely with the restaurant's ice cream offerings.

I ordered rice and green vegetables in a peanut sauce.

"I'll have fried rice, I suppose," said Jean. "Not much choice when you don't eat meat."

After our main courses, we both examined the latter third of the menu more closely. *Choklat, mocca, vanilie, buah*, and *plombiere* were a thousand rupiah, or fifty cents, each. An ice cream soda cost twenty-two hundred rupiah. Then there were a whole slew of delicacies priced between sixteen hundred and two thousand rupiah with names including Sony Boy, Moor Kus, Rococo, Nasal Rod, Nasal Rod Room, and OEN's Symphony.

"*Vanilie*," said Jean to the waiter.

"*Choklat*," I said.

Jean's verdict on the product, when it came, was precise and thorough. "It's crystallized. But you can't blame the manufacturer for that. They're not storing it correctly here." For the eight years prior to her travels Jean had managed and part-owned an ice cream business. "They use eggs. That's that other taste, that thick flavor in the back of the mouth. Surprisingly, considering they grow vanilla beans here, this is made with an artificial flavor. Vanilla ice cream should be very thin and light, and there should be no after-taste. This has a horrible after-taste."

"Other than that it's the best ice cream in Central Java," I replied. My chocolate had been fine. It had barely touched the palette long enough to register such refined sensations.

When the waiter returned to clear the table Jean asked how they stored all the twenty-seven listed flavors.

"No, no, no," he said. "This one," he pointed to the menu, "is two scoops of *vanilie* and one of *choklat*. And this is a *choklat* and two *vanilie*. This one," he indicated the Nasal Rod, "is a *plombiere* and a *buah* under a *mocca*."

"Hang on," said Jean. "How many flavors do you actually have here?"

"Five," said the waiter.

"Five!" I protested. "What about the OEN's Symphony?"

"One of each," he replied.

"And where's the Room?"

The waiter jogged over to his taxidermized elders at the bar and returned with a half-empty bottle of Bacardi.

After leaving the ice cream business Jean had taken a nine-month sabbatical. She worked as a gardener and came to realize how much stress she had been living under.

"I just couldn't imagine going back into business again," she says. "So when someone mentioned Bali, I thought, why not? and went to look it up on the map. Everyone thought I'd be away for just a few months, but I knew I was going for longer. I got rid of my possessions until what I needed fit into a backpack, and what I wanted to keep went in my sister's attic. I also became a yoga addict before leaving—I'd been thrown from a horse as a child and needed weekly chiropractic work. If I were to travel, I had to learn to take care of myself.

"When I arrived in Bali I ignored the taxi line at the airport, put my pack on and walked the three miles to Legian Beach. Legian was OK, but it didn't feel like Bali yet. The woman in the room next to mine was sleeping with two or three Balinese men a day. She thought I was crazy not to be taking advantage of the scene. 'So much nicer than Australian men', she said. I couldn't even sit on the beach and watch the sunset without someone coming up and asking me if I wanted sex. You know how you usually hear, 'You want room? You want transport?' Well they had an extra line: 'You want intercourse?' I repacked my bag and caught the next minibus for Ubud which the guidebook said was the cultural center of the island.

"I got off at the Ubud market place and started looking for lodgings in the rice fields that someone had recommended. People stopped me every ten yards offering to rent me a room. I kept saying no.

"Then there was this smiley Buddha-man sitting on a wall, just off the main street. He asked if he could help me. I told him where I wanted to go, but he said it was a long way away and that it wasn't safe to stay out in the rice fields anyway. 'Better you stay in a family house,' he said. 'Like at my brother's.' It was Darta. He took my bag and led me up a narrow dirt street lined with the front walls of family compounds. After a few hundred yards, we turned up a flight of stairs and went through a household's front gate. The gate was brand new and we walked in on its blessing ritual. The village priest sat cross-legged and surrounded by baskets full of offerings just inside the gate. He began saying his prayers just as I arrived. I was the first guest to walk through the new gate, and the first to stay in the new rooms Darta's family had built at the back of the compound. I knew as soon as I arrived that I had come home.

"Life on those back porches was very sweet. Darta came to teach me Indonesian everyday. I ate with the family, followed them to temple and watched the way they lived. Gradually, I let go of the fear and tension that had been knotted up inside me for as long as I could remember. Things started happening to me which made no sense to my businesswoman's way of thinking. For a start, people were sweet to me. At work I had always been the problem-solver and peacemaker. I had to deal with upset and angry people. Deep inside I found that I didn't trust anyone anymore. I had to let go of that way of being with people; it didn't fit with my new surroundings.

"Also there were nighttime things. It started with the feeling that I was being watched back in my room. Not a bad feeling, just that there was something there. It happened mostly while I was in the shower, and I often felt as if I were not alone while sitting on my porch at night. One night, well after midnight, I woke from a deep sleep with the feeling that I had to go and meet someone. Out on the porch I found a man sitting on the floor. He was dressed totally in black, with a black beret, and was smoking a cigarette. He had a weathered face. He was definitely there, but I could also see right through him. It was the first time I had ever seen a ghost, but it wasn't frightening. After that I started to see this old man more frequently.

"Another night I got up and walked down to the kitchen to get some water, and there he was again, sitting on the counter, smoking his cigarette. I could even smell the cloves. Then he said to me, 'Tell Suda to open the window.' I couldn't tell if he spoke in English or what, but I understood. Two nights later he was on my porch again with his 'Tell Suda to open the window.' The third time, I started talking back, 'You tell him to open the window,' I said. 'If I tell them about you, they'll think I'm crazy and throw me out!'

"I told the family then anyway. It seemed they should know. I remember starting to talk about the ghost to Darta as we sat on the kitchen step, and suddenly all the family gathered round. They started talking very excitedly in Balinese, which I couldn't yet understand, and then Darta asked me lots of questions about how the man looked: Was he happy or angry? Did he look healthy? Finally he explained that I had been seeing Roda, his dead father, who had always worn black, had smoked, and had his painting studio where my room had been built. I was amazed. They thanked me for the message and explained what it meant. The Balinese perform two cremation ceremonies for each body. The first, the big showy one that all the tourists go to see, breaks the links between body and soul. This had already been done for Roda. The family was still saving money for the second, smaller cremation that opens the way for the soul to leave this dimension and carry on towards its next incarnation. 'Open the window' meant 'Perform this second cremation as soon as possible!'

"I was really accepted as a part of the family after that. Ibu, Roda's widow, said that Roda had brought me to them. She said my arrival during the blessing ceremony for the new front gate was a sign from him since the new gate had been his last request. I went native then, wore sarongs all the time and almost stopped talking to Westerners. What a pill. But the family thought it was wonderful.

"I was doing a lot of yoga and meditation and they joked that I was some kind of a holy woman. Ibu, Suda and Darta were always finding new sacred places where I could meditate. On an auspicious day someone would take me by motorbike and leave me in a temple or under a tree for the night. Then they'd come and pick me up in the morning. I think they did this just to see what would happen. 'Will she go crazy or will she go into trance?'

"We started taking the whole family on weekend trips to holy spots after I bought them an old Mitsubishi minibus. It cost me three thousand dollars. They had some body work done and got it painted up until it was as white and shiny as new. Under the midday sun it was so bright you couldn't look at it. I called it 'White Cloud' and the name stuck. I was the only one who could drive it back then, and everyone's heads would turn to see a blonde Westerner driving all these Balinese around.

"I remember the first *Galungan* after we'd bought the car. *Galungan* is a big Balinese-Hindu holiday. The ancestral spirits come home for ten days and everyone prays in their family temple. The next day there's always a big ceremony at the important Pura Luhur temple on Batukau mountain, over in the west. It was a long, long way by public bus and few families had cars, so there were many people who wanted to come with us. As we started to leave, I turned around and counted heads. There were sixteen of us in an eight-seat van for what was then a three-hour drive. We were about to leave when Suti noticed an old man hobbling up the street waving his stick at us. It was her grandfather. He said, 'I'm old, and I've got a broken leg, but I want to go to Batukau before I die!' They hauled him up and in through the back window. He lay across everyone's laps all the way there. Then he had to walk two long miles from where we parked the car up through the forest to the temple.

"Sometimes we went to the beach and slept out. I taught them all how to swim and snorkel. At night the family would sleep on the beach while I sat meditating in some shrine or temple they had discovered for me. It was hard for me to stay out all night, though. Some of these places were really remote and I didn't want to scare any locals who might have found me in the morning. People weren't used to finding Westerners in their temples.

"Which reminds me: I have another ghost story that goes with the car and one of those trips to the beach. Suda had just learned to drive, and we were on our way back from the northwest coast with Chris, another long-termer at the family homestay. Suda was doing fine when suddenly, as we passed a big old tree and shrine, he started driving like a lunatic! At Tirtagangga we stopped for a swim in the freshwater pools. After that I said I'd drive the rest of the way home. Suda didn't care. He lay down in the back and went to sleep.

Chris sat with me up front, and I soon had this feeling that there was someone sitting between us. Chris felt it, too. 'What is it?' he asked. I glanced around and there, between us, was a little old man. He was both there and not there, just as Roda had been. He was dressed all in white, like a village priest. 'It's a little old man,' I said. 'Perhaps he's just riding with us for awhile.' I took another quick look and this time the man caught my eye. Then his whole face peeled open, revealing a long muzzle and sharp fangs. I looked away quickly. Chris said, 'Whatever it is, I think it should leave.' He said he couldn't see it, but he could feel it. We were right by the temple on top of the hill before you come down to Candi Dasa, where the cars stop for blessings. So I pulled up and Chris opened his door and jumped out. He held the door open and started bowing and inviting the spirit to step out. I sat where I was, thinking 'Go away!' thoughts. The ghost then got out of the car, dropped down onto all fours, and ran off into the bushes.

Suda then woke up. He asked us what we were doing and we told him what had happened. He said that he remembered he'd had a sudden urge to drive as fast as possible, but didn't know that he'd frightened us. We got our blessing from the temple and drove on. When we got home, Suda immediately called Ibu and his aunts together. They all asked Chris and I exactly what we'd seen: How was the old man dressed? When he showed his fangs, were they in his top or bottom jaw? Were his ears up or flat? Pointed or round? Which direction did he run off in? Where exactly did we pick him up? With every answer someone offered another name for what it had been. They took it all very seriously. They had dozens of names for all the different kinds of spirits. Once they were certain about what kind of spirit it had been, they knew what offerings to make to appease it and close the psychic hole through which it had been able to enter the car.

"Another time, at night, I saw a tall, huge being outside the front gate. It was bigger than the gate, hairy, and had long claws. It wanted to come in, but couldn't pass the gate and the offerings. Then I saw it again in the bamboo grove beside the compound. I was sitting on my porch and there it was, looking in over the wall. It wanted to get in, and I had the feeling that it could if it tried. I told Ibu, and she thought it was dangerous. The family spent a lot of money building a special shrine in that corner to keep such things out.

"It was a trippy time. I've never again seen the spirits as clearly as I did then. It was fun, for a while. I liked the idea of being a seer, but it could get a bit disturbing. What I did learn from the way the family reacted to it all was how limited my understanding of reality had been."

Jean's stay with the family became longer and longer. On a tourist visa, she had to leave the country every two months. Her passport began to fill with entry and exit stamps, both for Indonesia and its nearest neighbor, Singapore. One time she came back into Indonesia through Sumatra and went on a long jungle trek. It was on this trek that she met Eric, a Dutchman, who later became another long-term resident at Darta's homestay. Eventually, when Jean took Suda to see America for four months, Eric accompanied them.

"I was wondering how to return the hospitality the family had shown to me and thought of taking someone to the States. By that time, I had been living with the family on and off for two years. They had given me so much and been so generous in the way they shared their culture with me. I just wanted to give something back. I would have taken them all, but I couldn't afford to. Suda seemed as if he could best handle the experience, if a male friend came along with him. That was Eric's role. The whole idea was put on hold though when Suda's wife, Kadek, became pregnant with their second child. I put the trip out of my mind completely after the birth—Kadek's labor was so long and hard.

"At first she was taken to the local midwifery clinic. She was there all evening, but then her blood pressure plummeted in the early hours. She was rushed by ambulance to a hospital an hour away in the capital of Denpasar. I didn't go down then but came in later, at 5 a.m., with the van. I arrived to find Suda totally alone and distraught. He hadn't been allowed to see his wife and they hadn't given him any news of her condition. He grabbed hold of me: 'She can't die! She can't die! I couldn't live without her. She's such a good wife to me. So kind. She keeps the house clean. Keeps us all fed. Never complains...' They had made him sign a consent form for an operation and had then left him waiting. I barged my way through the red tape and in to see Kadek. By then she was very weak. I kept encouraging her to push just a little bit longer. Later, when I came out to tell Suda he had a new baby boy, he just turned on his heels and ran out of the hospital. I was just left standing there! Then, fifteen minutes later, he came back in, all done up in traditional dress with his sister Madé and her husband, Ardika, who lived nearby. He was smoking a cigar, they were all laughing, and he'd had his hair cut, too!

"As usual, the baby's grandmother went to a trance medium twelve days after his birth. Ibu was told that Adé was the reincarnation of her husband Roda. Apparently Kadek had been pregnant when Roda began talking to me in the kitchen about his second cremation. It all made perfect sense to the family: Roda had spoken to me because he needed to get out before he came back. He'd been cutting corners and trying to get back before he'd properly left.

"Soon after this I started dreaming about Japan. I couldn't understand why I kept having such vivid dreams. I was happy where I was. I didn't want to go anywhere. When I spoke about the dreams with the family, they said it probably meant I had to go to Japan. So I did. I spent almost all of my remaining money on a round-trip ticket, and arrived at Narita airport with just four hundred dollars to my name. It was late on a Sunday evening and there was no easy way of getting into the city, so I had to stay at a cheap, ninety-two dollar a night airport hotel. The cost didn't bother me though, even when I had to spend thirty dollars for the train ticket into Tokyo. 'At this rate I've got three days,' I thought, 'but You gave me all those dreams. I've got no idea why I'm here, so You take care of this.' I had this vague idea that I had been called to Japan to earn money so that I could take Suda to the States after all. I really didn't have any sort of plan, but within a week I had two good jobs, a place to live and had met my future husband. I had never, in my whole life, lived in such a state of trust before. And that trust was something I had found in Bali. So I guess it is possible to live what you learn."

The antiquated plumbing of the Hotel Oewa-Asia bumped and wheezed all night. It could have been some multi-fanged Javanese spirit for all we knew, but we were too tired to care.

In the morning we went down to sit on the hotel's front porch and have a breakfast of chocolate bread, hard-boiled eggs and super-sweet coffee. To meet the family, we had to get over the hill to the town of Ungaran. We asked the waiter for directions.

After packing and paying our bill we caught a minibus in front of the hotel and traveled across town to the bus terminal. No sooner had we arrived than a dozen young men descended on us offering to guide us to the correct bus. They were arguing with one another, pulling on our shirts, all forwarding a different opinion. They persisted even though we stood next to a bus with Ungaran listed among the destinations painted on its side.

"No, no, no, Sir. That bus over there." The young man was pointing to an empty bus. The bus before us was three-quarters full, running and had a driver behind the wheel. It sat under a sign which said it was the next bus to leave.

"Don't listen to him. He doesn't know anything. That other bus is the one you want." A bus with a sign stuck to the windscreen that read 'Jakarta' was indicated.

We moved toward the door of the bus that was about to leave. "No! Don't get on that one," everyone implored.

"Should we believe them?" asked Jean. "Maybe this one takes hours to get to Ungaran."

Above us, hanging out of one of the bus' windows, was an elderly man beckoning us to join him. Something stately in his demeanor made him instantly believable. Jean and I both noticed him at the same time. Our eyes met in accord, and we climbed on board.

We sat across the aisle from the gentleman and smiled at him, but he didn't say much. After exchanging pleasantries it became apparent that his Indonesian was too colloquial for us to understand. He did speak a little English however. When the ticket boy came by to collect our fare he instructed him, "You must speaking English. Ask them 'five-hundred,' not *lima ratus.*"

Upon leaving the terminal we drove back into the city, turning south toward high hills. The roads were a buzz with life. Semerang was very busy, but neither as busy and dirty nor as poor as Jakarta. Up a switchback out of the city we passed many bigger houses: former colonial dwellings taking advantage of the cooler altitudes. Half way up the hill we came upon the remains of a road accident. Everyone in the bus craned for a view. Slowly, we passed a very much over-heated minibus. Its body was a charred wreck, its tires were still burning fiercely. Surprisingly, there was no crowd of eager spectators. "Must be a regular occurrence," conjectured Jean.

There was no descent to make from the top of the hill; the road leveled out and began to follow a broad valley. We tried listening more closely to the ticket boy, not knowing where Ungaran was, but his calls were unintelligible to us. Roadside development had swallowed up the farmland between Semerang and its neighboring towns. We worried that we might miss our stop, but it was obvious. Just beyond a sign welcoming us to Ungaran, the bus stopped in front of the marketplace. From there we caught a horse-drawn cab.

The driver cracked the whip above the pony's ears, quickening the pace from trot to canter as the hill out of town steepened. The pony's hooves clattered against the road and the buggy lurched along in his wake. Not ten minutes from the market place we were already far from the smell of diesel fumes among hillsides of terraced rice fields and orchards.

The cab driver turned the pony and trap off the road and down a narrow lane to a small, secluded house. As we pulled up outside the gate, Darta's thirteen-year-old son, Abut, was playing in the yard. When he saw us he ran off to fetch his father and the rest of the family. By the time the driver had been paid, ten people were standing in the gateway, ready to great us.

"*Om Swastiastu*. May God be with you," the family chorused, bowing in unison with palms held together in a formal prayer of greeting. Abut stood in front of Darta and Suti with his ten-year-old sister, Tutut. Suda and Kadek stood with their nine-year-old daughter, Turia, and four-year-old son, Adé. Between the two families was Darta and Suda's sister Madé. Next to Darta was Pung, now a grown man.

It was Pung who came forward first, dissolving the formal atmosphere of the greeting into a melee of handshakes, hugs and laughter. Our bags were taken from us and we were led through the house's front door, down a short corridor and out into an open quadrangle. Our room was in the far corner, the women and children were beside us, and the men were across from them. We invited everyone to sit and talk, but the party lasted only as far as our door. The women, children and Pung disappeared and formality returned. We were left on our porch to drink coffee with Darta and Suda.

"Did you have a good trip? How are your parents? Siblings?" Re-acquaintance had its own particular formula. Even though the ice had been instantly broken, the complete ritual was still to be performed. We answered their questions with our news and then asked about Ibu and Rudy back in Bali, sister Ketut in Surabaya and brother Putu who worked as a policeman on the distant island of Flores. All were well and happy.

"How's Bali?" we asked.

"Same as ever," came the reply.

Next we were introduced to our host, Ibu Non, a portly, bespectacled Javanese Catholic nun. "She's Christian!" whispered Suda to me, like the religion was somehow contagious. Maybe it was. The family had arrived at three in the morning, after driving from Ketut's home in Surabaya through the traffic-free night. Perhaps a day full of Non's missionary zeal was weighing a little too heavily on their Hindu sensibilities.

But it was cultivation, not conversion we sought on that fertile hillside in the shadow of Mount Ungaran. Ibu Non was the driving force behind an organic farm project and a school that taught sustainable agriculture. We had read about it while still in Japan, and had then tried to persuade the family that some such scheme might breathe new life into the family rice fields. Their plot of land near the center of Ubud was already encircled by development. Within the foreseeable future the stream bringing water to their fields could be diverted, making rice farming impossible and leaving them with little option but to further develop. In a letter to the family we wrote, "We recently read that if all the airplanes coming to Bali were a hundred percent full, there would only be thirty percent occupancy in all the tourist accommodations on the island. Building more bungalows on the family land will be a waste of money. Better we look for another solution. How about you send Pung and Suda to Semerang to meet us and see this farm project?" We knew of one organic truck farm operating in Bali that did a roaring business selling to the beach resorts and Ubud restaurants. "There's plenty of room for another organic farm in Bali," we wrote. "The one already working can barely keep up with demand." In truth, it would be hard to maintain organic standards in the heart of Ubud, but Pung's family land in his home village was both plentiful and served by clear spring water. Our invitation to Ungaran had been met with great excitement. But it was the opportunity for the family to take its first "overseas" holiday, rather than organic farming, that had created the enthusiasm.

It was already after midday when Non invited us to lunch. In the kitchen we met some of the other staff. They had cooked us a lovely meal, but were too shy to talk. They just smiled or giggled. With our plates full, Jean and I thanked everyone, and then went to sit with the family. "Not a spoonful of fried rice in sight," I said. "This is wonderful!" Suda nodded a brief acknowledgment from behind a mountainous plateful of rice. When he stopped shoveling to take a breath, I asked him what they thought of the place.

"Ibu Non took us around the farm before she started class this morning. Very interesting." He was being polite. I had to fish for quite some time before getting a more honest opinion. "What they are doing here is what we did in Bali when I was a child." The inference being that it was old fashioned and backward.

Jean and I were a little disappointed by the family's reaction. "Just let it be," counseled Jean later. "I've seen this before. They take a long time to embrace new ideas."

Content that they had seen enough, the family was eager to get back on the road. They respected our desire to see the project we had been talking about for so long, however, and agreed to leave the next morning.

The farm was not large. We could have walked around everything in twenty minutes. Instead, we took all afternoon. The farm's basic function was as a training institute for people from the more remote Indonesian islands. "Many of our students have not been farmers before but must now grow their own food," explained Non. "Maybe they were forest people who now have no forest. Perhaps they're from a city where there's no work. Perhaps they live on marginal land, so their methods need to make the soil better, not worse. They come here for three months and study all aspects of sustainable agriculture. Our next group starts in another week."

Jean and I were still outdoors at sunset. We stood on the edge of a small wood, looking out across the valley towards the nearby volcanic peaks of the Dieng Plateau. From the town below, the wailing Islamic call to prayer was picked up by mosque after mosque. Broadcast from a dozen minarets over straining loudspeaker systems, the tape-recorded renditions vied for the attentions of both the faithful and Allah Himself.

"I've heard Darta describe it like this," said Jean. "The Javanese say that the Balinese, with all their colorful offerings, must think God is blind; the Balinese say that the Javanese must think God is deaf."

After dinner we sat with the family on the porch outside the rooms. Jean was right in the center, the honored guest, the children all over her. Over the time she had lived with the family strong bonds of love and shared history had developed. I was very grateful to have fallen into their company by way of marriage.

"We only have until Monday," said Darta. "Today is Friday, so we'll have a full day tomorrow. Then we have to drive back to Surabaya, spend the night, and drive on to Bali."

Jean nodded, apprehensive of the suggestion to come.

"How about this," said Darta. "Get up at 3 a.m., be at Borobudur for sunrise, then see Yogyakarta, Prambanan temple, and end the day in Solo?"

Jean and I locked eyes. We had counted on at least a week to complete that schedule. But the family had come so far to spend this time with us: How could we refuse them? We both took a deep breath. "Fine," we chorused.

CHAPTER 3

Possum Suda

Life in Java is impatient. It leaps out of bed at 4 a.m. From the moment the mosques begin to wail everything runs at full throttle. In the bedroom next door, the women began talking while the children played. Adé, never able to speak at anything less than a yell, was already making his mark on the morning. As daylight started to give definition to the world outside, he finally broke out of the bedroom and set off to wake the men in their room on the other side of the quadrangle. Jean and I were just grateful that we had been granted an hour more of sleep than we had expected. At six o'clock breakfast was served and by seven we were trying to fit eight adults and four children into a six seat mini-van.

"Where's the White Cloud?" I asked.

"She's getting old," said Darta. "She's having some time off, too."

Suda took the wheel. I sat beside him with Pung. In the second row sat Jean, Kadek and Darta. In the back, Suti and Madé bedded down amongst the luggage. The four kids were already blowing around the car like a small tornado.

Out on the open road any lingering cobwebs of sleep were soon blown away. The highways around the port of Semerang were already frighteningly busy. Long-distance buses raged by, overtaking whole streams of traffic. The drivers could not possibly know the road ahead was safe. When faced with oncoming traffic they just pushed back in. On the open road, might and nerve were right. Storming up the middle of the road, they devoured double white lines like maniac coke-heads.

Going uphill, our view of the road ahead was completely obscured by exhaust fumes. Suda slowed, aware of his precious cargo, and we were passed on both sides, beyond the white lines to our right and up the shoulder on our left. When we reached a fork in the road at the foot of a mountain, Suda turned right towards Yogyakarta. Within half an hour he had had enough. He pulled into the curb and turned to Jean.

"You should drive. You have thirty-five years more experience than me." He held out the keys for her.

"You can't be serious," said Jean. "I just arrived here three days ago. I haven't driven for months. What are you thinking?"

"He's thinking that anyone who's been driving since they were five must be able to handle this," said Darta.

The long-distance bus drivers granted no quarter to a blonde foreigner and continued to roar by like men possessed. The use of brakes seemed to tarnish their manhood, any flash of red being an embarrassing sign of weakness. Jean's response to such machismo was to ride the white line and the horn herself. This created the most room for escape, except when someone decided to pass on the inside at a critical moment. She drove like a matador fighting off a herd of crazed bulls. The required concentration completely excluded her from conversation. The conversation in the car completely ignored the danger we were all in.

We passed two dozen buses parked in front of a line of roadside food stalls. Signs in the buses' front windows reading 'Bandung-Yogyakarta' suggested this was a breakfast stop for the overnight run.

"Great," Jean said. "All those buses that passed us are now behind me again."

Pung took to pointing out things in the landscape that were the same as in Bali: kinds of tree, crops, the way the hillsides had been terraced. We crossed a bridge across a swollen and silt laden river. Pung turned up his nose. "Rivers here are always so dirty!" I couldn't decide whether he was being superior or homesick. The Balinese are very proud of their island and seldom stray far from its shores.

"It reminds me of northern California," said Suda matter-of-factly.

Jean turned and shot me a puzzled look, just to show that she was still listening. "California?" she mouthed.

"Where did you take him when you were there?" I asked.

"San Francisco, Mendocino, Yosemite. Nowhere that looks anything like this," she muttered.

I remember Jean telling me how golden the hills of California were going to be before my first trip home with her.

"They're not golden," I remember telling her as we drove north from San Francisco. "Wheat is golden. This is rain-starved grass. It's brown!" Perhaps we all see different images in the same picture.

After a series of slowly descending curves the road struck out from the base of the hills across open, cultivated land. Signs on buses began to announce routes to and from Borobudur. Ugly cement bunkers in the center of bulging towns began to sprout names like Beautiful Borobudur Hotel. "Definitely mutton dressed up as lamb," I said to Pung sitting next to me. He nodded politely, but remained confused. Idioms seldom translate into a foreign language.

In the back of the car the children had finally calmed down. Now that we were minutes away from our destination they begin to sing like little angels.

The Borobudur temple is vast. It is the world's largest Buddhist stupa. Over two-million cubic feet of stone were used in its construction. Its nine terraces are lined with hundreds of statues of the Buddha; terrace walls are carved with scenes from the Buddha's life. Much of central-Java's population labored through the eighth and ninth centuries to complete the structure only to have their Buddhist culture collapse after the stupa's completion. Buried by volcanic ash and overgrown by forest, the temple was forgotten for a thousand years until being rediscovered in 1814. Since its restoration it has become the site of annual Buddhist ceremonies. Most visitors, however, don't come to pray.

Borobudur has become a major tourist attraction for international and domestic holiday makers. It is busy at all times of the year, and especially so on a weekend.

Upon our arrival the whistles of smartly uniformed parking attendants directed us through long lines of parked cars and buses to a vacant spot. No sooner had we stopped moving than a troupe of hawkers descended on the car. Two arms came in through my window. One waved a plaster of Paris Buddha in my face. The other, while ostensibly waiting for payment, scoured the dashboard for valuables. Drink and sweet sellers opened the driver's door and pressed their goods upon Jean. The back doors were locked to keep the children in place but Darta and Kadek still had to close the windows to keep a rain of newspapers, plastic necklaces, bananas, and I-Love-Borobudur hats at bay.

Suti made the first move. She and Madé cracked open the hatch-back, rolled out, and quickly slammed it shut. Clutching purses to their chests they stood several yards away and bravely drew fire while the rest of us extracted ourselves from the car. The sellers steadfastly ignored Jean and me, concentrating all their energy on the Balinese. The family was polite but not forthcoming with their rupiah as we all shuffled across the car park towards the site entrance. Looking up beyond the gate and its attendant souvenir stands, and above a line of trees, we could see the distant top of the stupa. I must confess, the spectacle was a little disappointing.

Despite our guidebook's warning that the ninth-century Borobudur temple could be "crowded and noisy," I had been taken in by the idea that "the entire monument was conceived as a Buddhist vision of the cosmos in stone." Walking around the stupa's six lower terraces we would be "starting in the everyday world and spiraling up to nirvana—eternal nothingness, the Buddhist idea of heaven." From where we stood in the queue for tickets, however, it looked as though population pressures had forced nirvana to surrender a portion of its nothingness to the demands of progress. More immediately, we had to surrender a portion of our worldly wealth to the demands of the ticket seller.

"How much did you have to pay?" asked Suti as we regrouped beneath the trees.

"Four thousand rupiah each," said Jean.

"Ay! Expensive!" said Suti. "All of us got in for less than the two of you paid."

"Yes, but look at my souvenir ticket. It's so much prettier than your little scrap of paper." Foreigners often pay more than locals at tourist attractions. Darta and Suti always complain, claiming to the staff that we are "family." We tell them not to worry and regard the fee as a kind of wealth tax.

Beyond the trees we could see the whole stupa for the first time. Already robbed of its religious significance by the circus atmosphere, it resembled an enormously ornate, ten-story, gray stone wedding cake. Suda and the children left to ride a model train. At the foot of the stupa's first flight of stairs, Jean and I split from the rest of the group to explore the monument more thoroughly.

The carvings were impressive. Despite repairs that had put feet above heads and blank slabs of stone in the middle of elaborate panels, we could still follow the story. The spiritual atmosphere of the place was not strong, but we did feel the need to walk slowly, almost reverently, around all the terraces on our way to the top.

We were no more than a few steps into our pilgrimage when a group of young Javanese schoolgirls petitioned us for a picture. Actually, it was six pictures. Each girl had a camera, and each wanted their own record of the event. They posed around us like we were just another part of the statuary and, indeed, we felt a little stiff having to keep a smile up for so long. They left us standing there without a word of thanks or good-bye, gaily in search of their next photo opportunity.

Completing our circuit of the second terrace we looked down to see Kadek and Suti already on their way back to the car park. We worried that the family might already be leaving, and then heard Adé's voice somewhere above us. We later discovered that Suti had got all the way to the foot of the stairs before realizing she needed to go to the toilet. She and Kadek then walked back to the car park and the bathroom. "We got close enough to the stupa to see it," said Kadek, "so we went shopping instead."

The park P.A. system boomed a series of half-intelligible messages. A man at the foot of the stupa with a megaphone relayed these announcements, filling in the blanks for anyone within earshot. Both were drawing everyone's attention to the signs placed everywhere around the monument that required No Scratching and No Climbing. Rounding a corner, we came upon a couple perched next to a No Climbing sign on top of a wall. They were posing for a picture with a statue of the Buddha.

The Borobudur temple is crowned by three, broad, circular terraces lined with Buddha statues in conical shrines. There are good views and there is plenty of open space. Most visitors climbed straight to the top—hence the congestion in nirvana. Arriving at the top was like walking in on a big party. Hundreds of people stood around talking, playing with their children and generally having a good time. Many carried bright umbrellas against the fierce mid-morning sun. The colors made a festive contrast to the gray stone. A cloud of dragonflies that hung around the very pinnacle of the stupa's central spire added an exclamation point to the proceedings.

Suda and the children were among the crowd. "Come and touch a Buddha," Suda said, "for good luck." He was reaching in through the latticed masonry of one of the shrines. "You have to hold his hands. I can't reach, but you can. Then we'll touch you and get our luck that way."

As I reached in and took hold of the Buddha's calm, cool hands I was conscious of somehow reciprocating the action of the seller in the car park as he reached into the car with his little Buddha image. With Adé trying to squeeze as much luck, and perhaps blood, as possible from my other fingers, I looked at the statue's face and into its half-open eyes. I stared at five drops of dew that hung like tears in the corner of the eye closest to me. It seemed quite miraculous to have found such a bright liquid shining in the eye of a Buddha beneath the desiccating heat of the Javanese sun.

"Jean, look at this," I said. Soon we were all peering in at the mysterious drops of water. "Maybe it's from an insect."

"Yes, but what an incredible place for the insect to choose," said Jean. "Whichever way you look at it, it's amazing."

But Adé would not let us be at peace with our moment or ponder its message. He was at everyone's feet like a small animal, nipping at our heels for attention. Having secured it, he sat down in front of the shrine, crossed his legs, and placed his hands across his lap like a little Buddha.

"If only!" said his father, and everybody laughed.

Jean and I tried to take in the view and examine the statuary, but we had our work cut out satisfying the demand for our presence in people's happy holiday snapshots. Finally we had to start turning down invitations and retreat to a lower level.

Back in the park at the foot of the stupa we were again among the hawkers and vendors. On the path back to the parking lot we came across a pair of elephants, tramping around in a circle, carrying souvenir-laden tourists for two thousand rupiah a head. To a Balinese child who has heard of but never seen anything bigger than a cow, two whole elephants was almost too much to handle. "Elephant! Elephant! Elephant!" The children jumped up and down, pulling on Suda from every direction until he agreed to fork out the small fortune required to give them each a ride.

"How do you think we'll find the others among these crowds?" I asked Jean as Abut and Turia climbed onto their elephant. "I can't believe how many people are here."

"They'll all just turn up somewhere. They always do," said Jean confidently.

At a stall outside the gate we stopped with Suda and the kids for drinks. The foreigners stuck to the safety of Coca Cola. The children went for *es campur*, a cocktail of crushed ice, grated coconut, sweetened condensed milk, sugar and layers of black and green stringy jelly, doused with an indeterminable red juice and garnished with pineapple chunks. It looked more like the Brazilian flag than a drink. The rest of the adults filtered in from the surrounding stalls and ordered teas and coffees. We all amused ourselves watching a small group of American tourists at the next table stoically enduring the combined attentions of a sarong seller and a street musician.

"He's paying you to go, not to stay," called Suti to the singer. "Come over here where you're more welcome." Strumming his guitar and sending his beautiful voice before him, the young man came to serenade our table. "Watch Darta," Suti whispered to me. "He loves this kind of thing." And he did. He went all gooey and stared silently into space for as long as the musician played. Then Suti paid the man five hundred rupiah and we were on our way again.

Perhaps it was something in the words of the song, or a wish to remember the elephants, or some side-effect of the *es campur*, but everyone went on a mad shopping spree as we crossed the last few hundred yards to the car. Suda bought the children a plastic airplane on a stick, which Adé promptly commandeered, and a Borobudur T-shirt for himself. Pung got a T-shirt, too. Suti, ever practical, found some cakes and biscuits to see the children through the day ahead. Madé bought something, but I never saw it come out of its plastic bag. Darta didn't buy anything. He just went and stood by the car, still full of the ballad his wife's minstrel had sung for him. Kadek turned up last of all, triumphantly displaying her new gold-painted plaster of Paris Buddha.

It was 10 a.m. We had done Borobudur in a brief hour and a half. After standing around in the parking lot without apparent reason for a further ten minutes, we jumped in the car and roared off.

"You know," said Jean to Suda. "The last time we did anything like this together was in America." They sat together in the second row. Darta was driving, Pung and I beside him.

"I was thinking about that as well," said Suda. "Four years ago. That was the only time I was ever out of Indonesia."

"How long were we gone for?" asked Jean.

"After you'd been in Japan for six months you called and said you'd earned enough money for us to go America. You came back to Bali at the beginning of April, 1989. We left a couple of week later and we were in America for four months. I counted every day."

"Did you miss Bali?" I asked Suda. He was rarely in a mood to explore his State-side experiences. I jumped at the chance to find out more. "Did you miss your family?"

I turned to look at Suda. His eyes were wide with surprise. "Of course! It was so confusing to be away. Adé was just a few months old, so I was leaving a wife and a new baby. I missed my family terribly." He turned to Kadek. "Every night I had to play gamelan music and Balinese drama tapes before I could go to sleep. I was homesick and wanted to call home. I had promised to call Kadek every week at her office, but I could never get through to her."

"I was so upset," said Kadek. "After two weeks I went down to the telephone office in Denpasar. I went by bus. It took me two hours. Then I had to wait two more hours to reach Suda. 'Why haven't you called?' I said 'I didn't even know if you'd reached America alive or not!'"

"After that we set up times to call," said Suda. "She'd go down to Denpasar and call me collect."

Suda's journey to America began with a trip to the U.S. Consulate in Surabaya, Java, to get his visa. "The whole family came to the airport with us," said Suda. "Kadek was so sad to say goodbye. We were only to be gone a few days, but after that we would really be going."

"Suda played it wonderfully," said Jean. "He said his emotional farewells to everyone before pulling out extra tickets for Kadek and the kids. Once we were in Surabaya, I was very glad I had brought them."

"The clerk at the Consulate was very suspicious of me wanting to go to America with a blonde American. I just said, 'Why would I want to leave Bali and my family, to go to America?'"

"After Suda said that they just gave him the visa," said Jean.

"The flight across the Pacific was very exciting. The flight attendants kept giving me wonderful things."

"He took knives, forks, glasses, napkins, wipes, headphones, and kept stuffing them into his bag," said Jean. "I warned him that Customs might frown on his haul, so he put it all in my bag instead."

"Presents," said Suda sheepishly.

"When he wasn't looking I took them all out. It wasn't until much later, on a hot day in Santa Barbara, when I reached in my bag for the car keys, that I discovered he'd been collecting butter, too!"

"Stop! Stop!" howled Suda. "Don't embarrass me."

"After a few hours of the flight he curled up on the floor beneath my feet and fell asleep. Then he woke up, suddenly very frightened. 'What's that noise? It's like a monster. It's giving me nightmares.' It was the engines, of course."

"I was very nervous. I went to the back of the plane and found some other Indonesians to smoke with."

In Los Angeles Jean and Suda met up with Eric, the Dutchman who had also lived at the family home. Jean bought an old station wagon for five hundred dollars and they all went traveling. They drove up the coast to visit two of Jean's sisters in San Francisco, went on to Mendocino and back round through Yosemite.

"Suda and Eric couldn't smoke in either of my sister's houses, so they'd go out to the car for a cigarette. I'd come out and find them, windows rolled up. You could barely see them for the smoke. It was hard for Suda. So many things were totally unfamiliar. I understood his need to retreat to the car. Even back in nature, in Yosemite, where he thought he'd be OK, I was still on him. 'No Suda, you can't poop in the river. Here, dig a hole first.' He couldn't understand why he couldn't poop in the river. Every Balinese village has a river it uses as a toilet—at the top of the village it's for bathing and laundry, at the bottom for pooping. With fast flowing water and small communities, this system works for them, but it didn't work in Yosemite. I could only tell him that things were different in America."

"California was too cold, too," said Suda. "I was much happier when we got to Florida." Jean had two more siblings and her parents to visit in southwest Florida. She bought 'See America' tickets for her and Suda and they went flying around the country with Eric. "I remember," said Suda, "that one of your sister Kay's friends was just divorcing her husband."

"Not that things like that don't happen in Bali," interrupted Jean.

"But I was shocked at how many people in America bring up children on their own. Where are the uncles and aunts, the grandparents, the cousins, the second cousins? Even if the father disappears, in Bali there is still the rest of the family." He caught Jean's eye. They started laughing. "I know. Different in America."

"But you didn't know what different was until you went to Disneyworld, did you, Suda?" said Jean.

"Now, that was incredible!" said Suda shaking his head. "I remember it all very clearly. I think of that time often. What was the name of that part that I loved so much?"

"The Epcot Center," said Jean.

"Every building was a different place or a different culture. It was like visiting the whole world in a day. It was so real! No wonder America is so advanced. If only we had something like that in Bali that children could learn from. Then our country would make real economic progress!"

After Florida they visited Jean's sister Maureen and her husband, Craig, in Washington, D.C.

"We arrived in the middle of some house repairs," said Jean, "so Suda got to earn some money."

"Did I ever tell you about the monkey, William?" asked Suda.

"No, never," I said, though Jean often retold the story.

"Well, I was up on the garage roof, cutting back a big vine, when I found this big white monkey. 'Jean! Jean!' I shouted. 'There's a big white monkey asleep up here, shall I kill it?'" Suda was hopping up and down in his seat, reenacting the entire scene.

"I thought he was joking," said Jean. "But he was staring very intently at something. Then the foreman of the crew asked Suda what he was looking at."

"I said, 'A big, white, sleeping monkey!'"

"The foreman figured out that Suda had found a possum and tried to convince him that he should kill it. 'We'll cut it up, cook it right here on the barbecue,' the foreman said."

"Everyone was standing in the garden shouting at me to kill the monkey."

"I knew I had to do something quick to save the animal's life," said Jean. "Suda was salivating at the thought of freshly slaughtered meat—and Craig would've been no help. He served buffalo steaks while the Redskins played the Bills for the Superbowl! I was clutching at straws, but I could only think of one thing: 'Rabies!' I shouted. 'Possums carry rabies.'"

"I left it alone then."

"He came down real quick."

"After that day Craig always called me Possum Suda."

"I hear he called you lots of different names when he discovered what you did to his Playboy collection," I prompted.

"I never did anything," he protested, but his wide grin said otherwise.

Craig only discovered the crime weeks later, after Jean, Suda and Eric had returned to California. "Twenty-five years! Twenty-five years, Jean!" he said over the phone. "And not an issue missing. That collection was worth thousands. He took every centerfold. Every single centerfold!" They went with Suda all the way back to Bali where he sold them to all comers for a dollar fifty each.

"People don't collect things like that in Bali," said Suda. "There's no point. Everything molds. I just thought it was a pile of old magazines."

"Thought you said you hadn't done anything?" I said. Suda laughed. "Did you go from there straight to California?"

"No. Eric and I went to New York first."

"They gate-crashed a pensioners' day-trip to the Metropolitan Museum," said Jean. "It was cheaper than the public bus."

"We wanted to see the Statue of Liberty. We didn't have much money so we decided to take the old people's bus to the museum and then walk. It was a long walk to the ferry, and on the way we stopped for a beer. It was only later, when we were at the statue, that we realized we only had two dollars between us. It was four o'clock and the bus home was leaving in an hour. We already had our return ferry tickets but needed to take a taxi to catch the bus. I said we'd be all right but Eric told me two dollars wasn't enough. So we started asking people to help us, and got enough money together for a taxi. We caught the bus just in time!"

"What were you thinking?" said Jean. "When they got back to D.C. and told me the story, they said they had taken twenty-five dollars between them for the day and left without breakfast. The first thing they did in New York was get donuts and coffee. Then they had the beer. After hot dogs for lunch and the return ferry fares, they were lucky they got as far as they did! I'm sounding like their Mom. But it was like that. And Suda didn't always appreciate my mothering. He has a quick temper, but it's quick to pass. It was really wonderful seeing my country through his eyes, but by Washington I needed a break."

Suda and Eric went back to the west coast to do a week of gardening for Jean's sister Lyn. Jean stayed on with Maureen and

Craig. "A few days later I got a frantic call from Lyn. 'You have to come home right now. They've destroyed my garden!' Lyn had seen pictures of how beautiful Bali was and thought the Balinese must be great gardeners. So she asked Suda and Eric to clip a few of her trees and tidy up the hedges while she went off to work."

"I knew we had done something bad the moment Lyn got home," said Suda. "She looked at the garden, then burst into tears. But I had no idea what was wrong."

"They'd really worked hard. The huge limb of the old fig tree that kept neighbors from looking into the bedroom window: gone. The hundred-year-old climbing rose: hacked back to a stump. The two hundred irises planted the week before: dug up, and thrown on a huge bonfire along with everything else."

"I still feel bad about that. That's how we garden in Bali. Cut it back; it'll be big again in four months. Cut off a branch and stick it in the ground; it becomes a new tree. I didn't know any other way."

"From the building and the gardening you earned, what, two thousand dollars?" asked Jean.

"But before we came back to Bali I had to spend some of that on presents. I liked going to flea markets and garage sales. I bought lots of clothes. For Kadek I found an electric shaver I thought she could use for her legs. I still don't understand what it actually was."

"It was for shaving the fluff balls off sweaters," said Jean.

"People in America shave their clothes?" Suda sucked on his teeth and tapped on his head like he was checking the contents of a piggy bank. "I was so confused."

"But it wasn't all confusion," said Jean. "Some of the new things were exciting. One day we went to a department store and spent the day riding the escalators. It was so much fun. We shot two rolls of film, that's seventy shots of Suda in various poses going up and down an escalator."

"I have them in an album," said Suda. "But they look silly now. Almost all the new supermarkets in Denpasar have escalators."

"I chose Suda because he was the only one in the family who I thought could handle the intensity of all these experiences without changing. By that I mean that he would still be able to live as he had, in his family home in Bali. Someone else might have been seduced by the glamour of it all, or by the women—he's so handsome, they were after him all the time. He handled it all very diplomatically, and never strayed, either from Kadek or his culture. Every city we went to, he had me call the Indonesian consulate and get the addresses of any Balinese in the area. Then we went to see them. Many were wealthy people or those from higher castes that he would never have been able to meet in the same way in Bali."

"They were in America, and I was in America, too. We were equal there. Since then I have never again felt myself to be less than anyone else."

"Is that what you learned in the States then?" I asked.

"That, and how suspicious everyone is. The nicest people were suspicious of their friends and neighbors, even their husbands and wives! This was my strongest impression. People don't understand about trust in America, do they?"

Later Jean said to me. "I often wondered why I took him to America. I spent my last savings on that trip. Why did I do that? He says he's glad he went, but wouldn't do it again. Since he came back to Bali I've seen him become a village leader and gain respect: He's become really committed to his culture. I'm glad that someone in his position has had some experience of the West."

"Disney and all?"

"Disney and all," said Jean. "Some of his reflections might seem quite naive, but I think he saw things quite clearly."

"Does he have much influence in the village?"

"His position is really only as a public servant. He doesn't have much political power. He's seen how hard Westerners work to earn the money to come here, but others see tourists with lots of money and think that's how the West is."

"Suda doesn't spend much time with the tourists anymore, does he?" I said.

"Not like Darta, no. And not since he and Kadek ran the Cheap and Cheerful Café."

"What a fun place that was."

"And it was one of the few places where locals and Westerners ate together. But then Kadek's mother retired from her office job and took over the café. Since then, Suda's spent less and less time with the tourists and more and more time studying his own culture."

"Are you glad you took him to the States?"

"I'm happy that I was a part of his journey."

CHAPTER 4

Movie Animal

On the outskirts of Yogyakarta, Suda took over the driving once more. "Don't worry. I know where we're going," he reassured us as the countryside thinned and the traffic thickened. But it was fifteen years since he had been a university student in Yogyakarta. Things had changed. Every junction became an ecstasy of indecision and a bull-pit of conflicting opinion: "Left!", "Right!", "Straight on!" at the top of everyone's voices. Suda bravely tried to follow all advice, swerving this way and that in the middle of intersections until the press of traffic from behind forced him to go one way or the other. Only when safely beyond the point of no return would consensus erupt that we should have turned the other way. Blame for the mistake would then shoot around the car like a hot potato, either cooling over time or being reheated at the next intersection. When we actually ended up at the Kraton, the palace of the former Sultan, all the tribulations of the road were forgotten and there was much praise for Suda and his local knowledge.

As we entered the Kraton one of the official guides tagged onto our group. The family chose to deal with his presence by completely ignoring him. When we stopped in front of a large pavilion he explained that it was where the Sultan is viewed on three days each year. He carefully explained how the style and colors of the pillars combined both Hindu and Buddhist symbols, even though the Sultan had been a Moslem. He told us who in the court would have worn each of the costumes on display and pointed out the floors of marble from Italy and the lamps from Holland. He spoke a great deal and was very entertaining, but actually said little of substance. The family, however, was warming to him.

"I'm from Surabaya," he said, sensing the moment was ripe to turn from a stuffed shirt into human being, "but I've been in Yogya since I was this high." He tapped Abut on the shoulder. "My name is Gadot Sunaryo." He shook Darta's hand. By then we were standing in front of the gate to the inner palace. A picture of this entrance used to grace the back of the thousand-rupiah note. We lined up with the family while Sunaryo took our photo. "I prefer working with families much more than with big groups," he said. "Families can be much more friendly."

Next stop was the carriage collection in the palace museum. As in Windsor Castle or Buckingham Palace, there was an extensive exhibition of refined European carriage work and stately finery. Sunaryo was in his element.

The cut-crystal lamps and windows on the first carriage were pointed out to us. Suda stepped forward and wrapped on each pane in turn with his large gold ring. The sound seemed to please him. "*Bagus*," he nodded, "Good."

The next carriage was covered in gold leaf. We were told that it had to be drawn by eight perfectly white horses. Suda stepped forward and rubbed the ornate decorations on the door with his large gold ring. Apparently, they were authentic. "*Bagus*," he acknowledged.

Nearby sat an elderly gentleman on a small wooden chair. "This man drove the carriage for three sultans. He's now eighty-six years old!" exclaimed Sunaryo. I thought Suda was about to applaud as the old man drew himself slowly to his feet and bowed deeply. When upright once again he let rip a broad and toothless grin followed by an energetic thumbs up, and a single word: "*Bagus!*"

Back at the museum entrance Sunaryo surreptitiously pointed out the Sultan's younger brother collecting entrance fees. "Hard times," I thought, envisioning Prince Andrew checking people's bags at the Buckingham Palace gate.

"They no longer use the carriages for everyday travel," said

Sunaryo off-handedly. "Not since they got the Baby Bends."

"Baby Bends?" I said. The words evoked horrific images of small children in decompression chambers.

Pung rescued me from my confusion. "It's an expensive German car," he said.

"Oh! A Mercedes-Benz." Maybe the museum was more lucrative than it looked.

A five-minute drive away was the Sultan's water palace, Taman Sari. Sunaryo came with us in the car. Darta and the children followed in a three-wheel pedicab.

Inside the palace there were two pools separated by a suite of rooms and a low look-out tower. Sunaryo explained that the larger pool was where the palace women once came to bathe. The tower was the vantage from which the Sultan picked a beauty to come and bathe with him in the privacy of the second pool. Sunaryo continued his oration with gathering zeal, showing us the Sultan's dressing room, the lady's undressing room and finally the master bedroom. He showed us a tray beneath the palette bed. It had once held hot coals, adding to the fire of the Sultan's passion. When I pulled out my camera, a sign prohibiting photography was pointed out; the commoners were still obliged to turn a blind eye to the long-dead monarch's dalliances.

"I was in Bali last year," said Sunaryo to Darta. "I went to Tampaksiring, your Balinese water palace, where President Sukarno used to go to get his women." Sunaryo chuckled in the way that real men do about such things. "The Sultan and the President: both were playboys!"

"The palace in Ubud has a tower like this," said Darta, "overlooking the road to the market. The King would sit up there and pick women on their way to and from the market. He would use them once or twice, and then they would become servants in his household. My grandmother was very beautiful. My great-grandparents would never let her go shopping in case she was seen." Darta's expression revealed his fondness for his grandmother. "She would have been very confused in this city," he thought out loud. "I remember that she was so scared of cars. When they first came to Bali you could hear them on the road when they were still kilometers away. Things were quieter then. A car could still be on its way through the next village and my grandmother would refuse to cross the road in the center of Ubud!"

Sunaryo led us past the main pool, Pung shaking his head at all the plastic floating in the water. We walked out into a higgledy-piggledy district of low houses and narrow, winding streets. The neighborhood was built upon the remains of open waterways and secret underground chambers that had once been the palace pleasure gardens. Almost under the outer wall we went down a flight of stairs into a large, two story, circular chamber that had once served as a mosque. Sunaryo could tell us only that it was made long, long ago and that the tunnels had once run the twenty miles to the sea.

"Don't forget my name if you or your friends come again," said Sunaryo back at the car.

"Of course," said Darta.

"Last year I was the tourist in Bali, where you are the guide. Now I am the guide and you the tourist. I think that's funny."

Darta watched Sunaryo walk all the way down the street and around the corner.

"How much did you give him?" asked Suda.

"Five thousand rupiah."

Instantly the family factionalized into "you-paid-him-too-much" and "you-paid-him-too-little" camps. Their conversations sounded like a cat fight at the best of times. With a little venom added to the spice of their native temperament, things could get quite entertaining, sometimes even frightening, or simply exhausting, depending on how many times the fireworks happened in a day.

I walked over to the back of the car and pulled out a big two-gallon plastic flask of water. "Oh, don't do that," said Suti. "It's too heavy!" She left the discussion and came to help me. I am twice her size, but she took the flask from me anyway. She filled me a glass and I drank it down. She refilled it twice more. Jean always says that Suti is the incarnation of pure love. She is certainly devoted, selfless and unswerving in her service of others. I knew from long experience that there was no point in trying to do anything for myself that Suti thought she could do for me instead. She fussed and clucked, but in a most endearing way.

As I finished my third glass I heard Darta emphatically say, "If he comes to Bali, I will be his guide." Following such a magnanimous gesture, the heat of the disagreement instantly dispersed. Whichever way the karmic account stood, the willingness to rectify the balance had been stated, and that was enough.

Suda drove eastward from the Kraton as if he knew where he was going. Everyone else recognized this for the bravado that it was. Adé leapt back and forth between the back two rows of seats, driving the other children to and fro before him. We all knew him for the recalcitrant that he really was, and he didn't care.

"Get him away from me," squealed Tutut.

"Adé, you are so bad!" yelled his Mum, slapping the boy's rear end as it passed over her shoulder on its way to the back of the car where Madé was curled up feeling car sick. Adé's bottom, obviously affronted by this assault, somehow stopped in mid-flight to dance a little mocking jig across the top of the seat before disappearing from view. Kadek laughed, and I laughed with her. Her child was tirelessly naughty. "Where does he get it from?" she wondered.

Meanwhile Suda had spent half an hour driving three sides of a huge square. I could see the Kraton wall again in the middle distance. "Where are you going, *Bli*?" I asked, disguising my frustrations with his goose chase by politely addressing him as "older brother."

"Barbecued goat," he said, pulling into the curb. I sensed twelve pairs of saliva glands priming for action. "Oh!" Suda remembered. "You don't eat meat." Jean and I thanked the family for their consideration as we drove on. It was another five minutes before we parked before the open front of a *nasi campur* stall. *Nasi campur* is a staple dish: a mound of rice and a selection of miscellaneous vegetable and meat dishes. We were all ravenous. I ploughed in even though the food was spiced to a degree well beyond my taste. I ordered an extra half-order of rice and ate it on its own. There were enough spices burned into the lining of my mouth to flavor an offering twice the size.

"I don't think we'll have time to see the ruins at Prambanan," said Jean, sipping on her tea. Prambanan was the site of Indonesia's most extensive Hindu temple. "We'll probably go straight from here to Solo." She took another sip. "They're being very independent, you know." She pointed to the other end of the table. "Look at that. Darta's got a money belt on, like a proper tourist." Darta was scrabbling around inside his shirt, transferring funds to his wallet. "He told me they brought two hundred thousand rupiah spending money with them. That's a hundred dollars. And that's on top of the cost of renting this car. They usually fill their vacations with other work, but Darta said they should take the opportunity to bring all the kids to Java. He's big on them having as many experiences as possible. This holiday is a very big deal for them." The lunch stop was very brief. Jean had to leave half her tea. A meal was no reason to keep the road to Solo waiting.

At the next big junction, a beggar sat on the concrete island beneath the traffic lights. He held out his hands to the waiting traffic looking appropriately desperate. My Western eyes saw a young man, fine of limb and clear of skin. "What's he up to, begging," I thought. Suda's eyes saw things differently. As we drove by, a small handful of coins flashed out of the window and into the beggar's lap. I was reminded that, by Indonesian standards, the family was moderately wealthy.

The Prambanan temple complex, with its three imposing central shrines, lies just off the road to Solo. The parking lot was packed and the grounds were even busier than Borobudur had been. On the crowded footpath into the monument people started talking behind my back about how tall I was, unaware that I understood. After a full day of this my patience was running very thin. I just wanted to shout at them all to leave me alone. Finding a bench, I decided that sitting down would make me less obvious. It just turned me into a sitting duck for a group of women from Surabaya who cooed around me while running through half a roll of film. As they left me to discover the other attractions of Prambanan, Suda came to join me. "I see you've become a *binatang filem*, Will." *Binatang filem* means 'movie animal': A not-so-subtle pun on *bintang filem* which means movie star. I started to growl and Suda laughed.

Inside the temple proper, I pulled the guidebook out of my bag. I read that the temple complex had once covered a large area. Before me were three 150 feet high shrines, dedicated to Brahma, Vishnu and Shiva, respectively. In Prambanan's heyday there had also been two hundred and forty-four lesser temples, of which only two remain. All had been built during the eighth, ninth and tenth centuries. The complex began to fall into disrepair after Java's Hindu aristocracy—its princes, priesthood, artists, musicians, dancers—and their pantheon of deities all moved to eastern Java and then Bali, as their homeland converted to Islam. Most of the damage had been done by an earthquake in the mid-1500s. What stood before me was the result of modern restoration.

Climbing a flight of stairs into the interior of the central stupa's eastern chamber, I found myself in the presence of Ganesha, the elephant-headed god. We stood together, without other company, in the murk beneath the vaulted ceiling. The stupa had an atmosphere common to sacred places all over the world. Whether by virtue of some acoustic phenomena inherent in the geometry of the cell, or by some divine charisma emanating from the statue, or an enduring flavor from offerings long since past, I experienced a quieting of mind and a deepening and easing of my breath. Framed by the narrow doorway, the people of the world outside carried on with their lives as if in a scene from a movie. I drank in the peace and quiet as one would imbibe the cool waters of a high, clear mountain stream in springtime. I had maybe ten minutes of precious private time with Ganesha before a Chinese-Indonesian couple and their two dumpy kids ran me out, back into my proper role as the *"binatang filem."*

Sitting on the complex's low outer wall, I tried once more to take stock of my surroundings. Off to my left boomed the bass tones of heavy rock music. That this railed so directly against the spirit of our surroundings seemed to bother no one but me. A group of young teenagers emerged from a shrine, stereo in hand, and went happily on their way. They passed a group of nine girls who, to my horror, seemed to be walking directly towards me.

"Excuse me sir," said one of the girls in well-tutored but nervous English. She was the shortest in the gathering, was slightly heavy by slim Indonesian standards, wore glasses, and had her hair cut in a tight bob. She was not the one I would have picked at first glance as being the pluckiest in the group, but her courage was clearly gaining the admiration of her friends. Her manner was completely charming. "Where do you come from?" she asked.

"I'm from England," I said. Then in Indonesian, "And where are you from?"

"Ah! You can speak Indonesian!" The tension between us blew away on a passing riff from the Scorpions.

"Yes. But let's use English," I said, "so you can practice."

We asked each other: "Where are you going?" and "What do you do?" They were surprised that I had been to their hometown of Semerang, and the spokeswoman said that none of them had ever been to my destination of Bali. They were on a high school trip and nodded seriously when I said I was a writer.

"Are you married?" their spokeswoman asked through an enchanting blush. And then, "Will she be angry with us for talking to you?" I reassured them and wondered, without conclusion, about the cultural values that had framed such an expectation.

"What is your name?" was their last question.

"William," I said.

"William."

"William."

"William."

They all took turns committing the word to memory. I was less successful with their names. I remember only that the spokeswoman introduced herself as Lisa. "It's a short form of my full name," she said, "but it will be easier for you to remember." They had all turned to go when someone remembered the cameras.

They got the only pictures all day in which I offered a genuine smile.

We waited in the parking lot for at least as long as it had taken to tour the temple. We waited for Darta. When he came back, Kadek disappeared. We ate peanuts and drank water while sitting on the curb. Kadek came back and then Suda ran off with Adé. They came back fifteen minutes later, Adé clutching a new toy guitar.

The drive to Solo was relatively uneventful, save a panoramic sunset. Lulled into a false sense of security by this spectacle, Jean and I surrendered responsibility for finding a hotel to the family. The guidebook languished in my bag while Suda drove back and forth, round and round, looking for somewhere, anywhere, to stay. When we pulled up at the same set of traffic lights for the third time, Jean's patience ran out. She opened her door and stepped out onto the curb.

"I'm walking. I'll just follow you," she said from the sidewalk.

"But you don't know where we're going!" protested Suda.

"Neither do you!" snapped Jean.

Touché. Darta and Pung voted with their feet, getting out to stand with Jean. Suda nodded philosophically, conceding defeat. He got out of the car and joined them, too. The light turned green and a confused and angry snarl of traffic honked and squealed its way around our stationary, driverless vehicle.

A passer-by was politely accosted for information and we discovered that we were very close to a nice hotel. Jean, Darta and I chose to walk. Suda drove along beside us. We were soon joined by two locals, out for an evening stroll, who became interested in finding out how our little caravan would lodge itself for the night. "Sure, we'll walk with you. This way, that way—it makes no difference to us."

"I just couldn't take any more of it," Jean said to me. "Twelve hours in the back of that car with those kids climbing back and forth, screaming all those horrible songs and a space about the size of your notebook to sit in with Adé's stupid guitar digging into my side. I just can't do it again tomorrow." She was at the end of her rope.

Our short walk was over a mile long. For most of the way the imposing thirty-foot walls of Solo's Kraton towered over us. When we arrived at the hotel we found it was hosting a noisy wedding reception. The desk clerk told us they were completely full. Meanwhile, the women and children wandered straight through to the back of the hotel's open central quadrangle. There they found and installed themselves in three empty rooms. The clerk shrugged and signed us in. The men and boys took one room, the women and girls another. Jean and I were given a room to ourselves.

"There's a lot of them sleeping together," said Jean as we crossed the quadrangle. "I'm a little embarrassed that we're all alone."

"Come on," I said. "We haven't seen what they left us yet."

Peeling paint, naked light bulbs and an absence of bed linen are part of the definition of a "standard room" in such a hotel. We gave such conditions not a second thought. That the ceiling fan did not work; that there was no mosquito-netting over the windows; that the windowless bathroom had no light; that the walls of the bathroom echoed the clatter of several dozen pairs of little cockroach feet; and that the pile of garbage in the courtyard outside our door was topped by a very plump and healthy-looking rat: these were all added extras.

"I'm tempted to go and join the family," I said. "They may be forging a kind of safety in numbers."

We found the members of the family in their respective rooms in various states of repose. What they all had in common, whether they were laying on their room's double bed or the hard concrete floor, was that they had a layer of newspaper pages spread out beneath them.

"Any of that newspaper left?" I asked Pung.

"Sorry, Bli," he said.

"What are you doing down there on the floor," Jean asked.

"My turn."

"Oh, poor Pung."

"What do you mean, 'Poor Pung,'" said Suda. "Try sleeping up here on this horrible, hot foam mattress. He'd better lay quiet and enjoy the cool while he can. We're swapping in just two hours."

"What about you, Darta?" I asked.

"Oh, I'm happy anywhere. I brought my pillow." Darta's pillow is famous. When occasional guiding work takes him to Lombok, Java, or remote parts of Bali, the pillow always goes along. Darta claims that it has never been washed. "I won't allow it," he says. "It smells of my sweat and Suti's sweat, familiar farts and baby puke: all the comforts of home. A fresh or foreign bed is hard to sleep in, but with this under my head I'm OK anywhere!"

The women had developed a similar system to the men, except that they all shared the same double bed and rolled off onto the floor to cool off as required. "Like at the start of the hot season in Bali," said Suti. "Very uncomfortable at night with many bad spirits out and about looking to give people some sickness or other. That's when Ratu Gedé Macaling, the big demon from Nusa Penida island, comes to Bali to make trouble. He has terrible fangs. You don't ever want to see him. If you sleep on the floor like this he will think you're a pig or a dog, or that you're already dead. Certainly he won't think you're human, and then he'll leave you alone." Suti taught Balinese Hindu culture in a government elementary school. She imparted her pearl of knowledge to us with all the tender love, care and conviction that we had come to expect of her over the years. It was as if she was telling us to take this precious idea and store it carefully under "reasons for sleeping on the floor."

"Anyone hungry?" I asked.

We took pedicabs to the night market looking for somewhere to eat. There were half-a-dozen choices, none of which came up to the family's unarticulated standards. They procrastinated for so long that by the time hunger had lowered these standards to the point that choice was possible, there was only one place still open. Having ordered our simple fare everyone started whispering to each other how expensive the food was. The gossip was shared around the table in the same undertone with which news like

"He's got the clap!" would be passed along. When the food came, it was eaten in virtual silence. Suti had developed a headache, Kadek had a cold and Madé was still suffering from car sickness. The strain of the journey was showing on everyone.

Back at the hotel, the wedding reception was still dragging on. We had been gone for nearly two hours and the speeches were still in progress. Wishing each other good luck, we all retired to our respective quarters. With the lights out we heard cockroaches galloping around the bed and rats frolicking in the garbage. Bedbugs gnawed on our flesh. After the reception ended at about midnight, the men from the wedding party began a noisy game of cards directly across the courtyard from our door. They played until the first cocks crowed and the traffic began to run again.

Like survivors of a natural disaster, we all slowly emerged from the ruins of our night's sleep. We gathered on the benches and a low wall in front of the family rooms. Everyone looked like hell except Adé who, not surprisingly, had thrived on the atmosphere and slept well. While Jean and I sat on the wall, he came around behind us, pulling us by the shirt-tails to gain our attention. When we turned around to look down on him, he lifted both his hands above his head. He made an a O-shape with the thumb and forefinger of one hand and offered this gesture, with a nod, towards Jean. He pointed a rigid index finger at me and then brought the two symbols together, the one penetrating the other. He accompanied himself with a moist slurping sound.

"You little shit!" said Jean.

I aimed a slap at his little jigging backside. My hand wafted through thin air. He was already out of reach, running across the courtyard, laughing diabolically.

"Ay!" said Darta. "Last week he was at the supermarket in Denpasar with Suti and wanted a chocolate bar. Suti said no, so he reached up inside her dress and grabbed her pubic hair through her underwear. There's a Japanese woman who often stays with us—Adé does it to her, too. When she sees him she quickly goes the other way. And whenever someone asks him a question, about anything, he'll always answer 'Pubic hair,' no matter who asks him or what they ask. People are starting to call him Adé Pubic Hair!"

"Where does he get it from?" I wondered. My first thoughts were of the small room that Suda, Kadek and the children had shared for years at the family home in Ubud. Any child in such a household must receive a fairly complete sexual education at an early age. Next I thought about the family belief that Adé is the reincarnation of Darta's father, Nyoman Roda. One story in particular came to mind.

"Every hair on my head stood on end," says Kadek when she retells the tale. "Oh! Just thinking about it makes me shiver."

Sometime in the middle of his second year, when he was just learning to talk, Adé fell ill with a high fever. He was sleeping in his mother's arms among aunts, uncles and cousins as they all sat on the open pavilion in the center of the compound. Then he opened his eyes, pointed up to a faded and worm-eaten picture of Roda that hangs from a rafter, and said, "That was me before." Then he turned towards the kitchen, pointed to one of Roda's paintings and said, "I did that."

Hanging above the refrigerator in the family kitchen is a large canvas depicting a group of naked women by a river. In their midst is an ogre with a huge, erect penis about the size and texture of a coconut tree trunk. With this formidable weapon he is entering one of the bathing beauties from behind. The rest of the women, terrified, flee for their lives. The painting is of a scene from a traditional tale that warns against going to the river to bathe at midday. This picture is the first thing one sees upon entering the compound. When I first asked Darta's mother about it, she chuckled to herself, shook her head slightly, and said, "Ah yes. That was Roda."

Other pictures around the house are equally graphic. In one room hangs a piece, "The Penis Market," from another traditional tale about a village without men. The canvas depicts the scene around a market stall that sells erect horse penises. Like all of Roda's art, it is coarse and vulgar. It avoids being offensive only by its naiveté. When Westerners criticized his work, he replied, "This is what is in my mind, and in my heart. This is the expression of my soul." He claimed he did not paint for money, but sold almost everything he made, usually to the French. "They understand me," Roda said.

"Yes, Adé is like his grandfather," Darta postulates. "He is very porno, just as Roda was."

When I first met Adé he was still a babe in arms, barely a year old. Already the adjective most frequently spoken in his presence was *nakal*, or naughty. But in a Balinese baby naughtiness isn't generally seen as a problem. Naughty is synonymous with inquisitive, entertaining and boisterous. Reprimands for such behavior are always very half-hearted. For his first two or three years, Adé was adorably naughty. That is, until he got into his knife phase.

Knives are everywhere around a Balinese household. There are big kitchen knives, sickles of the field, and hatchets employed by the men during community work for purposes as diverse as whittling bamboo into string and butchering pig. Children usually learn to respect these honed edges from an early age. Adé learned that he could use them to instill terror.

I remember coming to the kitchen one lunch-time. Adé was chasing Kadek and Suti, a big blade as long as his forearm flying in circles around his head. He almost had them cornered, but they slipped by him and out into the open compound. As he pursued them around the garden their squeals of laughter were tinged with genuine fear. Finally, he got them where he wanted them, backed up against a wall. With his left hand he then pulled a flap of skin away from his neck. With his right, he ran the blade, slowly, menacingly across his own flesh. His mother and aunt were silent with horror. Then his uncle Darta walked in off the street, came up behind him, and whipped the knife out of his hand. Adé smiled up at Darta. Darta stared back coldly. Symbolically, he tapped the child's behind with his foot. Adé kept smiling up at Darta. They both knew he was immune to corporal punishment. "OK, Adé," said Darta. "Bath time." He quickly grabbed Adé's wrist and dragged the screaming, kicking, spitting fury of a child off toward the bathroom. Water was the only effective deterrent. Adé had an almost pathological dislike for it. Five minutes later Darta emerged, a little damp around the edges. He was followed by Adé, still fully dressed and soaked to the skin. Breaking away from Darta, he hastily ran to hide behind his mother's skirt.

As Jean and I sat on the wall in the hotel in Solo with Adé running circles around the car, I said to Darta, only half in jest, "Bli. Go get me a bucket of water."

CHAPTER 5

Solo in Solo

Once everyone was awake, we ransacked the car for a breakfast of biscuits, cake, bananas and apples. Madé went off to the hotel kitchen to procure us each a hot, tooth-shakingly sweet cup of coffee. We could hear her talking to the Javanese staff through the closed kitchen door and right across the courtyard. She has a voice with only two volume settings: loud and off. You talk to her across a room, or even across the entire compound, whenever possible. If you sit right next to her, you come away with bleeding ears.

"Madé seems to be over her car sickness," remarked Jean to Kadek.

"Ya. She slept well."

I thought of Madé's voice inside the confined space of the car. The prospect was frightening. "We're going to stay in Solo for a few days and follow you all back to Bali in about a week," I blurted. Sometime during the night, with the post-wedding card game still in full swing, Jean and I had talked about wanting to see Java a little more slowly, and in a little more comfort than was possible with the family. We had intended to talk with them before a final decision, but Madé's return to normal volume had put the issue beyond question. The cries of protest came as expected. Jean apologized, and pointed out that we would all be together again in Ubud in a few days.

It was Madé who accepted our decision on behalf of the family. "OK. You stay. But take good care of yourselves. And keep your bags close." Wise counsel for travel anywhere in the world, but that wasn't all she had meant. There was a touch of anti-Javanese sentiment, too. We heard it in the way she spoke and recognized it because it is common among the Balinese. It wasn't bare-faced racism, but it was prejudice, similar in intensity to the British mistrust of the French, and more an act of snobbery than anything else. The family had come a long way to explore their roots; Prambanan, Borobudur and the palace in Yogyakarta all represented important historical influences on Bali's culture. Though nominally Hindu, the island's culture is a melange of Hinduism, Buddhism and an indigenous animism. But with Java's Moslems outnumbering the Hindu Balinese sixty-five to one, Java's swelling population and Islam's missionary reputation are often cited by the Balinese as the biggest threats to their culture. Though far from being foremost among our reasons for continuing alone, Jean and I had talked about the family's attitude and wanted to see Java more clearly, with our own eyes.

The family did not depart immediately. They planned to spend the night with sister Ketut in Surabaya, visit an old Hindu site on Mount Semeru on Monday morning, and then head across to Bali. They did not have to leave Solo until midday. We all spent the morning at the Pasar Klewer batik market.

The Pasar Klewer is a two-story labyrinth housing hundreds of stalls. We arrived just as the shutters were going up. Madé, Suti and Kadek went swiftly about their business, mostly seeking presents for family members who hadn't come on the trip. I had my mind set on a nice batik that I could wear when going to temple with the family back in Bali. After half an hour of wandering around I decided which stall to buy from. I carefully picked a dozen pieces and had the seller spread them out across her counter. I was trying to pick the best one when Pung walked by.

"What do you think?" I asked. Pung shook his head almost sadly and sucked air through his teeth. "Well which one would you choose then?"

Ignoring the pieces I had accumulated, he smiled at the seller and pointed over her head. "That one," he said. The two-and-a-half by one-meter cloths had been folded down and piled up against the back of the stall, creating a floor to ceiling collage of inch-thick samples. "No. The next one down. Yes! That one." The seller deftly whipped out the cloth, theatrically flapping the piece open on the counter. Mostly black with a repeating floral pattern of light browns and deep blues, it was a far cry from the lighter pieces I had been contemplating. Pung took it, flipped it round my waist, and called to Suti at the next stall. She turned from the shirts she was contemplating, focused a brief but searingly critical stare on the proceedings, and said, "Perfect."

"Perfect?" I asked Jean.

She shrugged. "It does look good."

I turned back to Pung who looked me straight in the eye. His look said, "if you buy one of those other ones I won't be seen dead with you at a temple ceremony." Then he added, "I think you should buy this one, Bli."

I bargained hard, as I'd learned to do in Bali: Offer the seller no more than a third of the asking price; hold your ground while she mocks offense and drops the price a few percent; retort that your original offer was generous, even though she claims you'll bankrupt her. Enjoy the cut and thrust of the exchange, make sure there are a lot of laughs, pretend to leave, let the seller call you back, and finally agree to the sale at half the opening price. The Javanese seller started at eighteen thousand rupiah. I laid on the full show, but she didn't even give me a smile. She sold me the batik for ten thousand rupiah.

"That would've cost you thirty-five in Ubud," said Pung haughtily, flaring his nostrils at me.

"Is it good enough to go to temple in?" I asked.

Pung exhaled slowly. "Barely."

"Nah!" I said, throwing my arm around his shoulder. We both laughed. I knew as well as he did that he would graciously take me to temple even if I wore the cheapest, tattiest print I could find. But he was a fashion plate, come ceremony time, and would rather not have his image tarnished by association with a slob. We left the seller slapping everything in her stall with the crisp pink note I had given her. The first sale of the morning is believed to set the scene for the whole day's trading. The good luck symbolized by the money is thought to rub off on all the other goods.

We all wandered around the market for a long time, making the occasional purchase. Pung bought himself a shirt. Madé bought some things for her children. Jean bought a tablecloth and a matching set of napkins for my parents. From the market's second floor we saw Suda and Darta ordering an early lunch at a curbside food stall and went to join them. The women planned to eat and then return to the market, which convinced the men that it was time to go back to the hotel. "We'll follow you in pedicabs," said Suti, "but take all this stuff now in the car, won't you?" The men left, but Jean and I stayed put. We finished our meal and ordered a coke each, then rode home with the women once they were done with their shopping. By midday we were all stuck in front of a television in the hotel lobby watching an episode from an Indian version of the Ramayana epic.

"They planned their whole day around this, didn't they?" I asked Jean.

The war between the hero Rama and the evil Rawana, who had kidnapped Rama's wife, Sita, was reaching its climax. Considering the length of such serials, the war had probably been coming to a climax for quite some time. This particular episode retold the story of the battle between Rama and Rawana's brother, the giant Kumbakarna. The dubbing from the Hindi original to Indonesian was appalling. The effects did nothing to deserve the label "special", but the family was enthralled. After a lot of fist-shaking by the principal characters, Rama spent a few moments in deep meditation and uttered a few choice mantras to empower his magical weapons. He then loosed a volley of arrows which sliced the giant limb from limb. With Kumbakarna's head still screaming to itself in the desert sands, the end credits rolled. The family members then leapt to their feet and piled into the car. They were sad to leave us and were still worried that we were staying on to give them more room in the car.

"No, we want to stay. We want to see more of Java."

They meant it when they said they were sad, but they were being polite too, and they did look a lot more comfortable. "Let's go," said Suda. As the car turned the corner at the end of the street and disappeared around the end of the Kraton wall, we could still hear Madé's voice. She was telling Adé to watch where he put his guitar.

We took a pedicab from the line waiting outside the hotel and directed the driver to take us across town to the Westerners' Homestay. Tucked away down a maze of back alleys, it was quiet and clean. There were few formalities and we were shown straight to our room. Once the door closed, we flopped onto the bed and slept right through until sunset. We did not even unpack or undress.

When I awoke Jean had already gone to bathe. When she returned, I went for my own shower. On the drain cover in the corner of the small bathroom sat a heavy rock. I picked it up, looked it over and decided there was nothing special about it except its placement. We had put just such a stone on the drain in our bathroom in Japan to protect our bars of soap and our nights' sleep from a very persistent sewer rat. "Civilization the world over," I thought. "Just a skin-deep veneer."

We set out early for dinner, expecting to get lost. To reach the restaurant where we wanted to eat we had to make a long traverse across a number of city blocks via narrow, high-walled back-alleys and side-paths. We arrived without incident and had a leisurely meal. On our way home we were more relaxed and took the time to feel the atmosphere of our surroundings. Wandering down alleys between high, white-washed walls, we passed the occasional food stall with its complement of neighborhood personalities. Instead of the noise that might be expected from a regular crowd, people seemed reserved, almost lethargic. Perhaps this was due to the intimidating height of the alley walls or the way sound traveled.

Through low front windows there were glimpses into tidy, well-ordered lives. There were televisions, but of those that were on, none were blaring. In a small second-hand book and magazine store a dozen people stood quietly reading. Even the mosque we passed seemed to enjoy this same cloistered serenity. Through high, slit windows I was able to see several hundred men prostrated in prayer. The urge to take no more than a passing glimpse before hurrying on seemed an appropriate response to the sense of privacy inherent in the local architecture.

"I like this!" Jean said. "Java's nice!" She stated this as the revelation that it was. The back-alleys of Solo convinced us that we had been traveling too fast and perhaps had been experiencing little more of Java than the turbulence caused by our own passing.

Walking through the alleyways once more, early the next morning, we were struck by how clean everything was. The paths had been swept and the smells of coconut oil and cooking told us that the women were already busy in their kitchens. One of the small front rooms we had passed the night before was now doubling as a private English school, or so the sign proclaimed. Class had not yet begun. The book shop stood empty, too. Down a small side alley an arbor bowed under the weight of a brilliant purple bougainvillea. Glimpses through half-open gates exposed courtyards, both small and dirty, and wide and well-kept, with plants in pots and birds in cages. We passed a large gate with a brass plate bearing a doctor's name and walked to the end of the block without passing a break in the wall of his property. Around the corner were two families living in a lean-to propped up against the doctor's wall. At one of the small stalls, in front of an array of cheap biscuits, sweets and cigarettes sat a middle-aged man in a long sarong and faded T-shirt. Between his feet stood a little boy, naked from the waist down, all tears and noise from the neck up. "Good morning," said the man with a smile. The tops of walls already carried the harsh glare of full daylight while we walked in cool shadows. New whitewash contrasted with fading shades of gray. Brilliant emerald mosses enhanced truncated perspectives. It was a visual feast.

We took breakfast at the same restaurant we had sought out the night before. Across the wall was pasted a ten-foot by four-foot map of Indonesia. In the expansive scheme of the archipelago, Bali earned little more space than could have been covered by a silver dollar. "Where exactly are we right now?" I said to Jean.

"Solo's right in the middle of Java."

"And how shall we go on from here?"

"Well the guidebook says Malang is nice. And I'd like to visit the Hindu temple on Mount Semeru."

"I'd like to spend another day here, too."

"Let's travel the back roads, where we can. We'll take local buses and see Java."

"How long do you think it will take us to get to Bali like that? Four or five days?"

"I think so. I'm not as interested in the tourist sites as I am in seeing the country. And four or five days of public transport sounds like plenty!"

CHAPTER 6

The Temple to Mount Semeru

We spent a day and a half in Solo, wandering the streets and visiting the palaces and markets, before moving on. From Solo to Malang we took an afternoon tourist charter bus. The frequency of the high-speed, near head-on collisions kept us in a constant state of adrenal intoxication. We spent a day in Malang recovering. From Malang to Lumajang we opted for public transportation, reasoning that riding an older, slower bus would reduce the thrill value of the ride to manageable proportions. We were wrong, of course. A slower bus didn't take less risks, it was just slower at getting out of harm's way. Fortunately, the route we had chosen to Lumajang traveled a small mountain road through the foothills of the Mount Semeru volcano, Java's largest mountain. As the bus began to climb, the frequent twists and turns left little room for the driver to even contemplate overtaking.

From the road, we could see only the mountain's lower slopes. The twelve thousand foot peak was lost in a confusion of thick, gray storm clouds. In moments when the weather retreated, higher slopes, getting steeper and steeper, were revealed. Extrapolating from these brief glimpses, it was easier to imagine the mountain reaching upwards forever than to envision a summit.

I refocused my attention on the more mundane, taking note of the concrete statuary by the crossroads in most villages. Towering over one market place was a soldier supporting the slumped form of an injured comrade. The comrade was very green and definitely in a bad way, but it was hard to tell whether he was suffering from a gunshot wound or just a terrible case of dysentery. Into the plinth was carved the message: "Too much blood has been spilled." The statue clearly glorified nationalism and the post-war struggle for independence from the Dutch, but presumably the words also referred to the horrific bloodshed that swept the nation after the attempted coup d'état of 1965.

By the early 1960s, the Indonesian Communist Party was the third largest communist organization in the world. Only the parties in the Soviet Union and the Peoples' Republic of China had greater membership. President Sukarno, who had been in office since independence in 1945, relied on his ability to balance the opposing powers of the communists and the military to stay in office. Early in the morning of 1 October 1965, this game unraveled. Six top generals were murdered, the national radio station was seized and the Presidential Palace surrounded by a small force led by junior military officers with communist sympathies. In response to these actions, General Soeharto, head of the Strategic Reserve, mobilized the army and quelled the rebellion.

The results of this poorly organized attempt to seize control were far-reaching. A nationwide wave of anti-communist violence began in reaction to the attempted coup. Army units and armed civilians rounded up and killed all those suspected of communist sympathies. From the end of 1965 and through most of 1966, an estimated three to four hundred thousand people were killed. In the political arena, this blood-letting marked the beginning of the end of Sukarno's power, and the ascendancy of Soeharto. During the two years following the failed coup, communists were purged from all levels of the government and the military. At the end of March, 1968, Soeharto was formally inaugurated as president.

While the too-much-blood-has-been-spilled statue held up the current military regime as heroes and called for national unity, there was also a threat implicit in the propaganda. The statue left me wondering whether my blood was most likely to be spilled by militant rebels or a government crackdown. In another village a new concrete sign merely stated Indonesia's Independence Day, "17 August 1945."

A few miles later a ten-foot-tall cement hand raising the two-fingered victory salute was accompanied by the epigram: "Two is enough." This was a reference to the nation's family-planning policy. Statues of Mom, Dad, son and daughter all holding hands also promoted the goal of a small family.

Often we would see lists of the *Pancasila* principles and their respective symbols on which the Indonesian constitution is founded. These five principles—faith in God and the practices of humanity, nationalism, representative government and social justice—are symbolized by a star, a chain, a buffalo head, a banyan tree and twined sprays of rice and cotton.

"Let me off at the *Pancasila*," people would call to the driver when they reached their destination.

The bus emptied again as we climbed higher into less popu-lated areas. A change in the weather granted us a brief glimpse of the two horns of Semeru's summit. The view was impressive, but the mysterious mountain that had grown in my imagination had certainly been more so: Semeru, known by Javanese Hindus as the Mahameru, the Great Mountain; the parent of Mount Agung, the holiest of holies to the Balinese. I asked nearby passengers in the bus if they had ever climbed Semeru. All looked at me as if I were certifiable.

Our hotel in Lumajang was a short pedicab ride from the bus terminal. The receptionist was very polite, even speaking a little English, but he refused to acknowledge Jean in any way. When she spoke he ignored her, when she asked him questions he did not reply. He spoke to and looked only at me. I was led to the room; I was toured around the bathroom; he showed me the view from the only window out into the corridor; he told me about the curtain across the window that could be used to maintain privacy; and only I was offered food in the hotel restaurant. Jean was as invisible to him as the numerous large holes in the curtain and the balled-up pages of newspaper that filled them.

"Incredible!" said Jean, as he left.

After dinner and a short walk we met the hotel night watchman. His name was Augustinius. He had taught himself English and was obviously very bright. Under a jovial personality we felt the half-suppressed anger of one whose potential cannot be realized. He never said so directly, but he clearly wanted us to understand that Christians in Lumajang suffered from discrimination. We regarded him with warm sympathy.

"Have foreigners been here before?" Jean asked.

"Often," said Augustinius. "Dutch people come on holiday as part of a cycling tour that rides from here to Malang."

I tried, without success, to make connections between my ideas about cycling, my memories of the road we had just taken, and images evoked by the word holiday.

"Often," Jean reminded me, "means more than once. Or even only once if the impression left was strong enough."

The next morning we took a pedicab to the crossroads that was the terminal for the minibus up to the village of Senduro. Showing us the way was a new destination stenciled onto the road sign. It said, rather appropriately we felt, Pure, a variant spelling of the Balinese *pura*, meaning temple. It pointed our way to the Pura Mandara Giri Semeru Agung, the new Balinese Hindu temple honoring Mount Semeru.

We waited twenty minutes while the minibus filled and the driver's assistant strapped bicycles to the roof. Once on our way, we were soon passing through the outskirts of Lumajang. The road then began a steady climb through rice fields and small villages, offering spectacular views of the volcano's cone. It was not a fast ride. We stopped often to pick up or drop off passengers, and waited while their bicycles were added to or removed from the tangle on the roof. Minibuses passing us going the other way were mostly empty. Much of the downhill traffic preferred the cheaper, two-wheeled form of transportation.

By the time the minibus turned around at the top of its run, we were the only remaining passengers. We walked the few hundred meters up to the temple and, from the foot of the steps, looked up at the imposing, four-tiered stone gateway and its small pair of gilded wooden doors. We climbed the steps and tried the doors. They were locked. We walked around the wall and found a lesser entrance. A sign beside the closed gate read, "Enter only if you intend to pray." In a nearby pavilion a young man in a pair of jeans with a yellow temple sash tied around his waist was at work on a carpentry project.

"Ay! Good morning." His greeting was warm and open.

"Sorry," we said. "We don't have our temple dress, but would love to see the temple." We wore sashes and long trousers, but our sarongs were in the baggage we had given to the family to take directly to Bali.

"Ah! Don't worry," said the man. "But don't tell anyone I let you in."

He pushed the gate open and led us into the inner temple yard. Sitting on one of the pavilions was a priest dressed in white. We went over to him. We again apologized for our lack of proper dress and again asked permission to enter and pray. "Yes. Yes. Of course," he said. "You are welcome here."

Before us, across the courtyard and backed by tall green coconut trees, stood the high altar. To our left was the gateway we had first encountered, and to our right and behind us were a series of pavilions, each with intricately carved and gilded wooden pillars, beams and back panels. The compound was paved with large flagstones set into the ground a few inches apart with a hardy, green grass growing in between. In the grass stood several sticks of still-burning incense. Before each of these was a small, woven palm-leaf offering. Across the whole area were the scattered blooms and petals of marigold, rose and campaka; evidence of the pilgrims who had already visited the temple that morning.

In front of the high altar and between a pair of large ornamental umbrellas, two men sat cross-legged in prayer. Each was dressed in traditional temple attire. Folds of brown batik sarong cloth fell across their knees. Stiffly tailored white cotton shirts covered their straight backs. The sashes, which symbolically bind the body and its appetites, were obscured by the full length of these shirts. The cocky, white ceremonial head-dresses they wore, figuratively corralled their thoughts and directed them toward the gods. Across their seats and covering their laps were golden hip cloths, throwbacks to the time when everyone went shirtless and an extra cloth was worn to double as a blanket at night.

We walked over behind the two men and stepped out of our sandals. The warm flagstones and soft grass felt delightful under our feet. Using my sandals as a cushion, I sat cross-legged. Jean knelt, using her sandals as knee pads. The priest came over and gave us two sticks of incense, a box of matches, and a handful of assorted flowers and petals. He smiled apologetically. "I don't have any *canang* to offer you," he said. Without the usual small, woven palm-frond trays to hold our offerings, we were forced to improvise. We divided up the flowers and held them in our laps. I lit the incense, gave Jean a stick, and stuck mine into the turf between the flags in front of me.

I took a deep breath, drawing in the sweet, smoky fragrance. Passing my hands through a curling wisp of incense, I wafted the smoke toward myself in a ritual act of purification. Bringing my palms together, I raised them up before my forehead and closed my eyes. For me, the first prayer was a moment of centering. I let go of my preoccupation with bus routes and hotel room rates, acknowledged my place in the larger world, and allowed my usual sense of self to perforate. I embraced ritual time and magical space.

Opening my eyes, I lowered my hands and picked a tulip-like yellow flower from my lap. Cleansing it in the smoke, I pressed it between the tips of my middle fingers as I again brought my hands together before my closed eyes. I prayed to Brahma, the Creator, offering thanks for all that was in my life and suggesting a few additional creations. Always embarrassed to ask for something for myself first, I passed on to Brahma my specific wishes for the world, and for those around me. I prayed that the family had arrived safely in Ubud, I asked for a better job for Augustinius, I imagined a world without hunger or war. Then I asked that Jean and I be clearly shown what we were next to do, now that we had left Japan. Flipping the flower away, I let go of my prayer, sending its metaphorical vehicle on its way, unhanding the thoughts from which it was composed, leaving the slate clear, refreshed and renewed.

I picked up a blue hydrangea blossom. I prayed to Vishnu, the

Protector, who is said to have been born as Rama, prince of the Ramayana epic, and as Krishna who teaches yoga to the warrior Arjuna in the Mahabharata cycle. I asked Vishnu to bless my parents, family and friends. I took nearly ten minutes and imagined each of them, one by one, bathed in light and happiness.

Next, a frangipani bloom was held aloft for Shiva who dissolves and reforms all that is of this world, and brings death that is also rebirth and reincarnation. I viewed Shiva as a sort of cosmic compost heap, a rich source of new life. Brought up on stories drawn from the continuum between global warming and the Gaia Hypothesis, I felt closest to Shiva. I took his promise of renewal very seriously.

To be sure, my theology was not well read. It lacked bookish corners and sharp, scholarly edges. My beliefs and practices were born more of an inner urge to discover my own personal truth than of the impulse to conform to the orthodoxy of any particular creed. My last, empty-handed prayer reaffirmed my commitment to this inner urge, accepted myself as unable to maintain such an open state every waking moment of my normal life, and marked the end to this meditative ceremonial space.

We sat quietly until the priest came to stand before us with his tray and pitcher. He sprinkled holy water on our heads three times, then poured it into our cupped hands from which we drank, also three times. He poured twice for us to wash our heads, and sprinkled us three times more. Then he gave us each a few grains of dampened rice to press onto our foreheads, temples and throats. After applying the rice in the appropriate manner, some still remained. I took a single grain and chewed it slowly, consciously receiving it as the sacrament of the rite. I dropped the remainder on the ground.

The first time I had ever prayed at a Balinese temple was at Darta's behest. Jean had returned to Japan and I was alone in Ubud. I had been to every temple anniversary within walking distance of the family home since she had left, though I never actually partook in the rites. Usually I stood against the back wall soaking up the atmosphere, wandered among the stalls outside, or sat and watched the dance performances or shadow puppet plays. I had seen Jean pray with the family at certain times and was interested in exploring the experience for myself, but when Darta came up to me one night at a local temple ceremony and passed me a tray of offerings, I was suddenly possessed by a horrible fear.

"What's this?" I asked.

"If you want to go and pray you'll need these, and here are some matches."

"But what am I supposed to do?"

"Ah! You've seen us enough times."

"I don't know..."

"You know what people do. Go over there, around to the left behind that shrine. It's quiet there."

"But there are so many other Westerners here..." I was speaking to myself: Darta had already hurried off, back into the crowd. I suspected he was somewhat embarrassed to be seen inviting a tourist to pray, and I became intensely sensitive to any cultural mistakes I might make. I hurried forward, past the shrine that Darta had pointed out, to an obscure, empty corner of the temple courtyard beside the central shrines. Flipping off my sandals, I sat down quickly and began fumbling with the matches. I finally got the incense burning and hurried through my five supplications.

"Hi there everyone," I began. "You don't know me, but I'd really like to get to know all of You. I'm a foreigner in these parts and know very little about You, but I can certainly feel Your presence up there on the altar. I can feel the power here. And I'm really frightened of offending You all. So please, please treat me kindly because I haven't got a clue what I'm doing..." The longer I sat there, the more aware I became of the powerful atmosphere in the temple. "Oh, please don't strike me dead, God." It was almost pathetic. I managed to stumble through the prayers and the receiving of holy water and rice. Then I climbed back up onto wobbly feet while a group of women sitting on a nearby pavilion smiled at me and laughed. I winced a smile back and found the quickest way out of the temple and into the calm of the street. I walked back down to the family café and through to the back of the kitchen where I sat down and asked for a drink of water. When Pung handed me a glass, I gave him the tray of offerings.

"Just back from the temple?" he said.

I wanted to tell him to keep his voice down and not to tell anyone where I had just been. The fragment of my rational self still able to function justified this paranoia in the name of protecting the Balinese culture from too much tourism. "If everyone started praying here there would be no room for the Balinese," went the reasoning. In accordance with this desire not to encourage further tourist participation, or flaunt my own, I flicked away the symbols of my own transgression, removing every last grain of rice from my temples, forehead and throat. Then I remembered reading that the rice served as magical protection. To match the holy power invoked in the temple, there were apparently equal draughts of evil swarming the streets around and about. Immediately I became acutely aware of this dark and malevolent presence. It dripped from the rafters, sucked at the soles of my feet, and screamed in my ears, teasing out each and every primal fear. I had to get away, and quickly walked, almost ran, all the way back to my room. There I locked all the doors, lit incense again, and shivered under the blankets for hours like a five-year-old until exhaustion finally allowed me to drift into sleep.

I was very glad to wake with the first light of day and find that the emotional storm had passed. Over breakfast I talked to Darta about my experience. He made the following clear to me: First, I had been invited to pray by a member of the local community who had been moved to do so by the spirit of the occasion. By implication, therefore, I had actually been invited by the gods themselves to pray. Second, the atmosphere of the occasion, whether formed by the focused intent of the villagers or by the presence of some kind of deity, had been full of acceptance and laughter. Finally, a temple ceremony is about communion and community, love and connection. There was no room anywhere in this scenario for the terror I had experienced.

"Well, if it didn't come from out there," I concluded, "it must have come from in here!" I had been near mortally frightened of my own shadow, and this was a great revelation to me. As I reviewed the evening's events, I gleaned far greater insight into my own culture than I did into Bali's culture. Clearly, the wrathful God I had shivered before was of my own projection. And if this God really was in the temple, as my actions supposed, then outside of His home I was bound to find a kind of hell. Further confusion had been added by my seeking this quasi-Christian God in such a pagan way. Religion and God had barely ever been mentioned throughout my upbringing, but somehow this latent Christianity had surfaced. Having been to church only for the occasional wedding, I had thought myself immune to the bindings of religion, yet there I had been, the original sinner. Coming to me as it had, the experience seemed to be almost entirely the result of personal and cultural bias. My beliefs had become manifest in a shocking way while simultaneously showing me that a different theology made for a very different world view.

On another occasion, I attended the cremation of one of Darta's in-laws. It was a huge community event with more than twenty different sarcophagi waiting to be burned. Some were made in the shape of black bulls, most were winged red lions, and there was the occasional simply decorated box. There was also a most eccentric elephant-headed fish. Most of the ten-foot-high constructions faced east or north, but there were a couple that pointed westwards.

"Why is there such a mix of styles here?" I asked. "I thought there were set ways to perform this ceremony." I was already mindful of Darta's all-encompassing caveat that everything in Bali varied according to time, location and situation.

"Well, it is usual for lower-caste Sudra families to use the red lion and for the black bull to be reserved for the Wesia and Satria castes. It is also usual for the casket to face east toward the sunrise or north toward Mount Agung, the Mother mountain. But these are not hard-and-fast rules. My in-laws, for example, while being Sudras, use a black bull because it is a tradition on that side of the family." I stood close by while the wrapped remains of three recently exhumed family members were placed inside the belly of the bull along with numerous offerings. Gallons of holy water from various earthenware jars were then emptied into the sarcophagus. The attention of the thirty or so family members present and the devotion of the songs the women sang in the old tongue were intently focused on the ritual. "So long as they believe in what they are doing," said Darta as the fire was lit, "it will have the desired effect."

"Darta, is that a little skepticism I hear in your voice?"

"Certainly not! It's just that we Balinese understand the relationship between what we do and what we mean by what we do. We can seldom give you good reasons for why we do what we do—for example, why do we need to make five of these offerings on this day and one of those on the next? I don't know—but we know what the offering is meant for. When we concentrate on making an offering that meaning becomes part of the offering, and that is enough for it to work."

"So, if you believe it, it works?"

"Of course. Ah! William, I know how you think. 'We don't always get what we ask for,' you say. 'So how do we know the offering works?' But you have to look at the bigger picture, the macrocosmos. Think about karma, the laws of cause and effect. Words are one thing, but what do your actions say? The mouth is always talking and talking, but what are your hands and feet asking for? Na! There are your beliefs and there is your world."

"So making the offering turns our actions and our thoughts in the right direction."

"Precisely."

"But, Darta, is it only about karma and what we do in the world? You believe in God too, don't you?"

"Ya. When we talk intellectually, we talk about karma. We can be very scientific. But when we look in a spiritual way it's all very confusing. Understanding karma doesn't help us to know when and where our karma will come back to us. That's still a mystery. So we make our offerings, and we go to the temple and pray."

Many pagan prayers since that first night in Ubud, I sat on the warm flagstones of the Pura Mandara Giri Semeru Agung, smoke still curling upward from the incense before me. The priest was sitting on the pavilion again. He had been joined by a second priest and the two men with whom we had been praying. When we stood up, they all motioned for us to join them.

"Hello," said the priest who gave us the flowers. "Would you like a cigarette?"

"No thank you." I said as we sat down. "But these are your matches, and thank you for the offerings." The priest took the matches and lit himself a cigarette. "May I ask your name?" I continued.

"My name is Jero Mangku Misto." He spoke very slowly as if talking to a young child. This did not feel condescending, I was grateful to hear the words clearly. *Jero* is an honorific, *mangku* means priest and Misto was his given name. The other priest was called Jero Mangku Satomah.

I then turned to the two men we had been praying with. Ida Bagus Disa came from east Bali. The *Ida Bagus* marked him as being from the highest caste, the Brahmana. Disa was his given name. He said he had been at the temple for five months, overseeing the finishing touches of its construction. With him was Ida Bagus Paramarta, also from east Bali, who accompanied his name with his entire address. "Pura Mandara Giri Semeru Agung, Senduro, Lumajang, East Java."

"You live here now?" said Jean.

"Until the end of July, yes."

"Where are you staying?"

"Right here. Just down the street."

"Are you from Bali, too?" I asked Misto.

"No!" He coughed out a big cloud of cigarette smoke as he laughed. "There are many Hindus around here. I live just one and a half kilometers down the road."

I turned toward Satomah. "I'm from Pandansari," he said. "About four kilometers from here."

In a corner by one of the pillars lay the donation book and box. Jean picked up the book and only had to flip back one page to find familiar names: Suti had given five thousand rupiah; Darta had donated fifteen thousand rupiah. Jean added our names to the list and twenty thousand rupiah, about ten dollars, to the collection.

"This is a new temple, isn't it?" she asked.

"Yes," said Misto. "Very new."

"Have there been any ceremonies yet?"

"No. Not yet. The first ceremony is at the beginning of July." This new Balinese temple in Java had been all the conversation within the family when we had first met them in Ungaran. Both for reasons of religious pride and mystical significance, the building of the temple at the foot of Java's highest mountain was considered to be of great importance. Our visit had been to find out what all the excitement was about.

"The event will last eleven days," said Satomah.

"Oh, a big ceremony," said Jean.

"Of course. We have to give people a chance to get all the way here from Bali."

"This is now an important temple," said Paramarta. "Water is taken from here for the temple ceremonies at Besakih, the Mother temple on Bali's Mount Agung."

"There's a holy spring here, too?"

"Well, not right here. Ten kilometers by car and another four by foot."

"And that's close enough?"

"Close enough."

"Why was the temple built here then, in this village, and not at the spring?"

"Well, we could have built the temple anywhere. Nothing stopping that," said Misto, taking another deep draw on his cigarette. "But there was a stone found here that marked this as an old Hindu site."

"And, if you don't mind us asking," I said, "who paid for all of this?"

"Most of the money came from Bali. Donations were received by the Bali Post, and Ubud contributed a lot of money." No wonder the family had been proud. "A number of local Moslems heard about the temple and wanted to help. Some gave up to a million rupiah."

I asked who had built the temple and we were told that the basic work had been done by local labor. The fine woodwork and stone carving had been done by craftsmen from the Balinese regency of Gianyar, of which Ubud was a part.

"Do you get many tourists coming up here?"

"Oh yes. Many," said Disa.

"What kind of people?"

"Well, there was a Dutch cycling group, as I recall."

"Ya, I remember them." said Paramarta. "They came through here—when was that?"

Back out on the street we were confronted by a large black-and-white sign, in English, which we had failed to notice on our way in. It read, in capital letters:

CLEANLINESS IS NEXT TO GODLINESS

"Is that talking to us?" I asked Jean.

"We both had showers this morning. Can't be."

"I don't think enough tourists come this way for them to be worried about litter louts."

"And anyway, it's the locals who throw their plastic all over the place."

"Especially during a temple ceremony. All the sellers along the street. All the thousands of offerings in the temple, swept up and thrown over the back wall to compost. That's a lot of trash."

Up the street a little further was the construction sight of a new hotel, obviously aimed at housing pilgrims from Bali. The barrack-style rooms were about half complete. Quantity, not quality, was clearly the dominant design criteria. A sign announced forty-six rooms, with prices in the fifteen to twenty thousand rupiah-a-night range, to be opened by July. In their frantic efforts to complete the project before the temple ceremony, the builders had turned the entire site into a deep quagmire.

"The village stands to do well because of this temple," said Jean. "But their peace and quiet will definitely be compromised. Perhaps the sign was put up by the local anti-Hindu faction!" The very idea of such an organization seemed absurd to the point of being hilarious.

We were the only passengers in the minibus for most of the bus ride back into Lumajang. After an early lunch we checked out of the hotel and began another hair-raising bus journey to the east coast town of Banyuwangi. We spent the night there and, in the morning, took a ferry across the narrow Bali Strait. By late afternoon we were back in Ubud at the family house, sitting on the porch of our usual room.

CHAPTER 7

Adé's Birthday

In the half-state between full sleep and waking, in the moment between seamless eternity and temporal experience, where the senses are still distant and muted, and awareness remains expansive and impersonal, it feels as if a choice could be made. But it never is. The mere cognition of choice plunges one back into sensory reality.

When one tricks oneself out of sleep in such a way, it is nice to wake in a familiar bed. Morning light is always more refreshing and reassuring when drawn from a well-known palette and seen through well-known frames. Familiar sounds and smells from beyond the bedroom door, and well-known voices, near enough to comfort, far enough away to leave one undisturbed: All these things ease the transition from night to day.

I rolled over toward Jean. She was looking at me.

"Good to be back." Her voice was barely a whisper.

I nodded.

"Coffee?" she asked.

I nodded again.

Neither of us said anything more. We dressed and went out onto the porch. I moved the two bamboo chairs and the coffee table to one side. Jean got the broom from its nail behind the corner pillar and swept the floor. I took the cushions from the chairs and dropped them onto the floor for us to sit on. We made hot, black, bitter coffee from the flask of hot water on the table and sat looking down the path toward the kitchen, watching the family we had come to love as our own as they went about their business.

"Yes. It's good to be back," I said.

We went for a walk before breakfast. Just a brief one around the village. We could have gone uphill, out of the village and across the rice terraces that surround Ubud, but from the front gate we turned left and walked the three hundred meters down to the main road. The family compound was one of many that lined a narrow lane. On either side of us were the front walls and roofed gates of other households. Before almost all of these gates hung signs announcing "homestay" accommodations. Most gates and walls were overhung by the lush foliage of trees and garden plants. The street was green and pleasant, though the shade was less than it had been during my first visit in 1989. New power and telephone lines had required the cutting of many trees.

At the bottom of the lane were a pair of huge shade trees around a pond full of lotus flowers. There also was the courtyard of the temple to Brahma. Had we turned right on the main road, towards the western end of the village, we would have passed a number of restaurants and souvenir shops before coming to the long flight of steps up a hill to the Temple of the Dead, dedicated to Shiva. Instead, we turned left, passed Brahma's temple and the village hall, and came to the main crossroads. To the east of the crossroads, on the main road, were the market-place on the right and the palace of the village's prince on the left. Though the royal family had ceded power to the national government upon the formation of Indonesia after the Second World War, the prince still enjoyed considerable influence over village affairs. The first courtyard of his palace was also the enchanting venue for the nightly traditional music-and-dance performances laid on for the tourists.

Running south from the crossroads was Monkey Forest Road. When Jean and I were first in Bali, this road had still been bordered by rice fields. Now it was the central tourist area for

Ubud, lined with hotels, shops and restaurants. At the bottom of the road, about a mile from the crossroads, was a small wood and an overly-friendly troupe of monkeys. There also was the Temple of the Dead and the cremation ground of the next village, Padangtegal.

The road north from Ubud's main crossroads was the one street that had escaped significant tourist development. Opposite the palace was a large banyan tree. There were few homestay signs and only three restaurants. The furthest north of these was the Cheap and Cheerful Café, and that was only three hundred yards from the crossroads. Almost opposite the café was the temple, closely associated with the village's royal family, where I had first prayed at a Balinese ceremony. Another half-mile up the road was the village temple to Vishnu. A quarter of the way to this was a small alley to the left which took us back to the family house. As we walked in through the front gate, Ibu asked us if we were ready for breakfast.

"Yes," said Jean. "That walk gave me an appetite. Can we eat back on our porch, Ibu?"

Lolet brought us breakfast. Five years before, he had been young enough to sleep in my lap as I wrote letters on my porch in the afternoon. He was a cousin from Roda's side of the family tree who had lived with the family for so long he was regarded as the fifth brother. Back in our old, familiar Bali-morning routine, it seemed as if some stroke of magic had quite suddenly turned him into a handsome teenager. Our years in Japan seemed a distant dream, almost as if they had happened to someone else. I touched the simple band of gold around my ring finger to remind me that they hadn't. Even the story Darta began telling to the couple on the next porch took me back to those first, fresh Balinese mornings.

"What does Ubud mean? It comes from the old Balinese *obad* which means medicine. Na, when the first expedition came here from the old Hindu empire in Java, Bali was still mostly jungle, a very difficult place. There were diseases and wild animals, and good water was hard to find. Most of those people died. Only a few made it back to Java.

"When the second expedition came it was a little better prepared, but it still found Bali to be a very hard place. After many months and many deaths, the remaining members of the expedition were very sick. Then they came down to a place where two rivers met at the foot of a hill. There was fresh spring water to drink, so they stopped to rest for a few days. Many who had been ill got better very quickly, and so they believed that the place had special healing powers. They set up a small shrine and made offerings of thanks to the local gods. Then they traveled north to the place where Taro village now is. That shrine by the river is where we now have the Campuhan temple, and this area has been known for its medicine ever since. All the villages for about five kilometers in every direction go to Campuhan in big processions at the start of any temple ceremony to collect holy water.

"Na. Many, many, many years later, Ubud was a small village in the rice fields. Just a few hundred people. Nothing like what you see today. There wasn't even a palace; no princes, only farmers. It may be hard for you to understand, but the Balinese can be a very fierce people and it was very hard to live without the protection of a prince. Nearby villages all had their palaces, but Ubud had nothing and the people were often very hungry. My grandfather's grandfather was one of the village leaders at that time. When the village council decided to go and ask the prince of nearby Peliatan for one of his sons to be the prince of Ubud, it was my great-great-grandfather who went as head of the delegation. He was received very politely by the king, who listened carefully to his request. But the king said, 'I'm very sorry. All my sons are gone. I have only four sons: one is the prince here, and the others are now the princes of Mas, Petulu and Batuan. There is no one left to give to your village.'

"My great-great-grandfather was disappointed, but thanked the king for his time. Then, when he was already out on the street, the king's first minister came running out to request that the delegation come back to talk with the king again.

"The king said, 'I forgot someone. My first son. But I don't know where he is. If you can find him you can have him.' The king had once made one of the palace serving girls pregnant; so he was not an actual prince, but good enough.

"The men of Ubud then went out to find their new prince. They spent many, many months and looked everywhere for him. Eventually he was found way up near Mount Batur, living in a lean-to under a betel-nut tree. They brought him back to Ubud, gave him a house to live in, and called him Tjokorda Beten Buah, or The Prince Who Lived Under The Betel Nut Tree. But giving him a house and a name didn't stop anyone from feeling hungry, so the Tjokorda sent one of his new ministers to ask his half-brother in Batuan for some rice. When the prince in Batuan heard the request, he became so angry that he said, 'Your prince isn't even a real prince! He offends our family name by coming like a beggar. He wants something from me, I'll give him something. But not rice. I'll give him the sharp edge of my kris!' When the minister told the Tjokorda back in Ubud that he had better get ready for war, the Tjokorda said, 'Better to die with honor in battle than to die slowly of starvation.'

"I don't know if anyone actually died in the war, sometimes when two sides lined up for fighting and drew their weapons, just the magical power of one side's krisses was enough to cause the other side to turn and run. Anyway, Ubud won. And in Bali at that time, winners took everything! The people of Ubud went down to Batuan and took everything they could carry from the palace. We still have one of their wooden *kulkul* bells in the village banyan tree. North Ubud community rings it when there has been a death. Also, the prince of Batuan's land then belonged to the prince of Ubud. And that wasn't the end of the fighting either. Ubud won another war and took over many, many rice fields near what is now Denpasar. The royal family in Ubud was then very, very rich!

"Na. But in Bali there is always balance. When you are rich you have to give very big ceremonies and help with the temples. Every time the royal family had a wedding or cremation they had to sell land to pay for it. They did this right up until recently, until the Tjokorda had almost no money left and only a few small pieces of land that everyone thought were worthless. You see, everything in Bali is about balance. What goes up must come down. So the only land the royal family had left was a few rice fields and steep ground by the river. But the Tjokorda was still very respected and still a leader of the village, even though he wasn't so rich anymore. Then someone bought the royal family's land by the river to build a hotel on. I heard they paid many, many millions of dollars for all that land that had only been good for growing grass for roofs! Now the prince has three Mercedes! Very, very rich again."

Jean spoke to me in a low voice. "Have you heard that story before?"

"Of course."

"If he's telling that story, this couple must've been here about two weeks."

"C'mon! You make it sound like he's following a curriculum."

"No. Well, maybe something like that. But isn't it wonderful the way he makes the same old stories sound fresh every time? When he told them to me I was sure he'd never told another soul before."

"The mark of a gifted storyteller."

The couple next door got up from the porch and followed Darta. They were going to the pavilion in the walled family temple to see an old earthenware jar taken as spoils of war from the palace in Batuan. Passing our porch, Darta stopped to say, "And this is perhaps the most expensive hotel room in the world."

"I told you we should have negotiated harder!" I said to Jean. We hadn't negotiated at all when we arrived. If we argued with Darta over the room price it was always because we wanted him to accept more than he asked of us. We often had a hard time making him take any money at all.

"A woman walked in here late one night and rented a room," Darta continued. "She paid me and went back to her room. Ten minutes later she was banging on my door in a panic. She said she was lost and had rented my room because she couldn't find her own homestay. She said she had to get home and asked for my help. She said, 'There was a big gate and a black dog,' which didn't help because all houses have gates and dogs. It took me three hours walking with her to find her real homestay, three doors away down the street! Anyway, I kept her money, of course: fifteen thousand rupiah for less than ten minutes. That's equal to a daily rate of twelve hundred dollars. Very expensive." The tour moved on towards the kitchen.

"I've heard that Ubud story before," I said to Jean, "but I've never seen the Batuan jar."

"Well, go follow them then."

The four tourist rooms were against the eastern wall of the compound. The porches overlooked the precincts of the family temple with its pavilion for the making and storing of offerings and its shrines. The path in front of the porches ran along the low back wall of this temple, past the well-head and through a dense garden of ferns, frangipanis, hibiscus, and stunted conifers. In front of our room it turned toward the kitchen and the front gate. I followed Darta and the two tourists as they walked past the temple and the kitchen into the open center of the compound.

Around us were the buildings of the family home: the *balé dauh*, the *balé daja* and the *balé dangin*; literally the Western Pavilion, the Northern Pavilion and the Eastern Pavilion.

The Western Pavilion backed onto the road. Made of brick and tile-roofed, it had a small, open porch and was divided into four small rooms. About a dozen people slept there, including immediate-family members, cousins, second-cousins, and friends of the family. The Northern Pavilion was built in the same style, though it had only two bedrooms and a verandah that ran the full width of the building.

The Eastern Pavilion was much smaller than the other two. It had six wooden pillars, a thatched roof, and was divided by a curtain behind which was a raised wooden palette that served both as an extra bed and an altar on which to place offerings during certain ceremonies. This back area was walled in on two sides. Guests were received in the front half of the pavilion, where they sat on the tiled floor and had an open view of the whole compound.

The kitchen was a step across the path from the Eastern Pavilion. It had a covered porch where everyone squatted to eat. Off the porch was a tiny passage where a twin-burner gas cooker stood on a cement counter. At the end of the passage was the original wood-burning stove.

The foundation of each of these four buildings was built to a different height: the further east and the further north the building, the more auspicious it was and the higher it stood. The wide steps up onto every pavilion functioned as the household's armchairs and sofas. The center of the compound was, quite literally, its living room.

We followed Darta back round to the gate into the family temple. "Please wait here," he said. "You see that I am wearing a sarong and that you are not, so only I can go in. I will bring the pot out here. While you wait, you can look at our Northern Pavilion. This is where a family's virgins sleep. If any boy wants to sneak in to make love with one of the girls in the middle of the night, he has to pass all the family sleeping in the front rooms and the old grandparents who usually sleep on the Eastern Pavilion. If he wakes anyone other than the girl, he has to go out again past everyone else's knives!" Darta crouched over, set his face into a snarl, and mimed stabbing the male tourist in the guts. "Think about it while you wait," he said. "Natural contraception. We've only had condoms here since 1962."

Darta loved to shock people. He left us with the man still holding his stomach and me laughing inside. A few moments passed before he emerged again holding a simple, clear-glazed clay jar, about fourteen inches in diameter and maybe twice as deep. Darta continued his theater by stopping any of us from touching the pot. "Sacred," he said.

I'm sure the tour of the compound could have continued, but a neighbor then came in and asked Darta to move his car.

"Just like old times," said Jean back on the porch.

Rice was ready in the kitchen and Darta's mother, Ibu, signaled us to come and eat. "No one should eat anything in the morning before a good plate of rice," she said as we joined her.

"I'm still full from breakfast, Ibu," said Jean. "But I know William will eat." With a fruit salad and a slim banana pancake to whet my appetite, I was always ready for the eleven o'clock brunch that Balinese eat as one of their two meals a day. We sat on the tiled floor of the Eastern Pavilion beneath a photo of Roda as I ate.

"Darta's really a man who's found his vocation, isn't he?" I said to Jean. "Can you imagine how miserable he would have been as a lawyer?"

"I don't think anyone really expected him to be one," said Jean. "When Roda was diagnosed with liver cancer, he refused treatment. He insisted that Darta, Madé and Suda finish their university education instead of paying hospital bills. 'Spend the money on the living,' he said. 'And don't expect good jobs or lots of money from your education, just learn to tell the difference between right and wrong.'"

"Adé must be suffering from a little inter-incarnational amnesia then," I quipped.

As we finished eating, Suti came to sit with us.

"No school today?" I asked.

"Sunday," she said. She wanted to hear about our travels across Java. She hung on to our every word as we described the palace in Solo, the day we spent in Malang, and the various bus rides we had taken. She was delighted that we had managed to visit the temple on Mount Semeru. When Darta returned, she sat him down on the kitchen step and re-told him our news. She was about to finish when a tourist wandered in off the street. We recognized him as one of the other guests, a young Finn who had chosen an ascetic life on a mountain top in a remote corner of Australia. He was well over six feet tall, pale and skinny as a bean pole. He wore a skimpy yellow singlet and blue tights, but no underwear. He was dragging a ten-foot-long banana leaf and walked right through the middle of our conversation on his way back to the rooms.

"What was that, Jean?" said Darta.

Jean laughed and shrugged. "I don't know. We'll have to ask him," she said. "Excuse me! Excuse me." The young man turned towards us and returned her smile. "What's the leaf for?"

"I eat at the food stalls at the night market, and I know it's dirty." He spoke slowly and with a strong accent. "When I carry the leaf with me, I always have a clean plate."

"Oh yes," said Jean. "Thank you."

The Finn left, but Darta's eye's remained wild with surprise. "Who was that? Is he staying here?"

"I'm sorry," said Suti, laughing. "I gave him the room last night." When Suti laughs, her voice is soft and hoarse. She waves a hand at you, especially if you've made her laugh at someone else's expense, and tries to stop herself, though she can't keep a straight face. "It's my fault. I always attract these people."

"It's true," said Darta. "When I was courting her, she worked at a food stall in the market."

"All the strangest people came to eat at my stall. Everyone else sent them away, but I couldn't. I felt sorry for them. There was one man who bought one cup of coffee and then sat on my bench with it all morning. He never even drank it. And then there was the man who came to me every day without any sarong or underwear on. I just served him like he was any other customer. Other people laughed, but my heart went out to him."

That afternoon we wandered across town to the family rice fields where Suda had his house. Since my first visit to Bali he had built a house for himself, his family and Pung. We arrived in time to watch him win a game of chess.

"Local champion," said his opponent.

After his friend left, we sat with Suda in idle conversation. Pung joined us, as did Kadek once she returned from work. Over coffee and sweet rice cakes, we filled the hours until dusk.

Taking our leave, we walked home on a big loop through the paddies beneath the changing colors of a broad equatorial sky. Near the end of the walk we stopped and sat to watch the sunset, then had to feel our way down the path through deeply shadowed woods toward the family home.

"When Suti was very pregnant with Abut, she didn't sleep well." We were having a late brunch with Darta, and somehow the storyteller had been set off on one of his tangents. Suti had just returned from teaching school. She changed from a skirt into a sarong and came to sit by Jean. "One night," said Darta, "Suti heard someone out on the street below the bedroom window calling her name. 'Ti! Ti!' So she woke me and I went to the window to see who it was." Darta put his whole body into a tale. He showed us how he lumbered out of bed and across to the window. "The road was empty. But Suti's brother's child was very sick, so we assumed there was some big problem. We got dressed and hurried down the street to his house. When we got there we found all the doors shut and all the lights out. No one was awake and none of the children were crying. We woke Suti's brother, but he said he hadn't been by. We got very scared on the way home. Who had been calling Suti's name? Perhaps a witch, or a ghost that can disguise itself as a woman, a dog, or a pig. And then there it was—coming down the road toward us—a big pig!"

"'It's a witch!' I whispered," said Suti.

"I said to Suti, 'Get down! Get down, woman!' You must squat down low when you see a witch. My uncle Paman saw them often in his village, and people see them all the time at the river. You get low to show respect, then they won't disturb you."

"But I was too pregnant to squat. 'I can't! I can't!' I said. So I just stood there and thought lowly thoughts. I was very quiet. The witch kept on coming right down the road straight toward us. Then it stopped right beside me."

"What happened!" Jean was on the edge of her step.

"It trotted off down the road and disappeared round the corner," said Suti.

"It didn't do anything to you?"

"No. It was just a pig."

"How did you know?"

"You just know," she said offhandedly.

"Next morning," said Darta, "our neighbor was round looking for his lost pig. Neither of us said anything. We were too embarrassed to say that we'd seen his pig, that it had walked right by us, and that we'd done nothing."

The Balinese are not always that placid in the face of real or imagined threats, however. Later that afternoon there was a near-lynching in the market-place. We did not see it but could hear the crowd all the way up at the family house.

A man, an older woman and a younger woman had robbed a jewelry shop, but the alarm had been raised before they had made their getaway. They were caught by an angry mob on the street. The crowd beat them severely and would have killed them had not the police waded in to take charge. Later, a villager who had been there told us how they had stamped on the old woman's head. "But there was no sign of blood! None at all! It must have been magic," he said. Darta confirmed that the woman had been wearing a protective amulet.

With the perpetrators whisked off to the police station, the crowd's growing anger was turned upon the thieves' brand new Toyota. The mob broke the windows, ripped off the doors, tore away the tires, peeled off the bodywork, and smashed the chassis.

"I saw it later," said Darta. "There was nothing left. My cousin had just set up her stall for the night market when all this happened. Everyone came and took the pipes that made up her tent and the cement blocks she used to anchor the ropes. They used it all to attack the car." He shook his head and chuckled. "She lost everything! She'd been renting that equipment for a thousand rupiah a day because she couldn't afford to buy it. But now she has to replace it, so she's bankrupt." Darta's attitude seemed to be that his cousin's loss was a reasonable price to pay for the safety of the village.

Jean and I sat on our porch talking late into the night. Rumor had it that the thieves had confessed to being members of a large gang. The same rumor held that they were receiving some rough treatment at the police station in Gianyar and were being beaten for more information.

"How did that news get here from Gianyar?" I wondered. "Just a tall story?"

"Maybe," said Jean. "But they're better off there than they would have been if the police hadn't arrived. The crowd on the street would've killed them. That's the Balinese way of dealing with crime."

"Summary execution?"

"Traditionally, each village governed and policed itself. When the Gianyar police interfere, they still have to show Ubud that traditional justice is being done."

"This is just a story to appease Ubud then?" I said. "I wouldn't be surprised if they really were beating them. After all, they were Javanese."

"You're right. There is a fair amount of prejudice going on in all of this." Some were viewing the daring daylight raid as a slur against Ubud's cultural integrity. "Vigilante law is hardly just, but it seems to work here."

"It worked in the past, perhaps, when you knew everyone else in the village and understood their characters. The outsider was automatically suspect. But Ubud isn't a closed community anymore. There are thousands of out-of-towners working here with the tourists."

"Jean, William, are you still talking about the robbery?" Pung's voice preceded him up the path through the darkness.

"What do you think about what happened today at the market?" I asked as Pung sat down between us.

Pung sucked air through his teeth, but would not be baited into a discussion. "This is not my village. It would be different in my village," was his reply.

"How?" asked Jean.

"Well, we don't have any jewelry shops. There's almost nothing anyone would want to steal in my village. If there were any problems, they would be within the community and would be dealt with by the community."

"What problems might there be?"

He then explained about the stealing of water. Rice farmers organize their growing seasons and the movement of water between fields communally. Diverting irrigation waters to your own paddies at the expense of others can be an offense under traditional law. We asked him about rape, murder and kidnapping, but, in the context of his village, he found such ideas confusing and hard to grasp. Such crimes happened elsewhere.

"Do they happen in Ubud?" I asked.

"What happened today is very unusual," he said, getting up to leave. "It won't happen again."

Night falls quickly in the tropics, and with it come the spirits of the night. Dawn is like a lamp going on and marks the return of our world. Daylight and darkness are intimates, and twilight is a veil across which they may reach and touch each other. Birth is frequent within an extended family and the rituals accompanying new life always involve the slaughter of pigs, chickens, ducks. At temple anniversaries the altars are covered with offerings to the gods. Every fifteen days smoldering coconut husks are put out for the demons. Night and day, birth and death, good and evil, creation and destruction—all go hand in hand for the Balinese. Life is about balancing these opposites.

For Adé Pubic Hair, whose reputation had spread far beyond the four walls of his family home, it was clear that some serious rebalancing was called for.

"It's his *oton*," said Ibu. His *oton* was his birthday according to the 210-day Balinese calendar. "We're going to do a special ceremony to purify him."

The sun was three-quarters of the way across the sky, and the Eastern Pavilion was laden with offerings. A few weeks previously Kadek and Ibu had been to ask a local trance medium about the preparations for such a ceremony. They had been given a long, hand-written list outlining the offerings to be used. They had been told how many old Chinese coins to include, that only perfectly white eggs should be used, and that a black chick was required.

"All this because he is so naughty," said Darta.

One of the village priests was coming to conduct an extensive purification prior to the usual small ceremony performed on the occasion of a child's *oton*. That morning, water had been collected from twelve springs. Nine different colors of flowers and nine different colors of fruits had also been gathered. These were combined with the woven palm-leaf offerings the women of the family had been working on for the last week. A pair of deep-fried chickens, crucified on a pair of crossed skewers, completed the arrangement.

Ibu and her eldest sister-in-law, Ibu Teku, a tall and regal woman with long, white hair and no teeth, sat on the kitchen floor waiting for the priest. I was with Darta and Kadek on the steps of the Eastern Pavilion, and Adé was asleep in his mother's lap when Jean returned from the market. She had bought Adé some birthday presents: a new child's sarong, yellow hip cloth, white head cloth, and white dress shirt. Usually he made do with folded-down versions of adult temple wear. "To help Adé become less naughty," said Jean, handing the packet to Kadek.

"Let's hope so," Kadek said, then woke her child and took him off to one of the bedrooms to change. A few minutes later he emerged in his new finery. He loved it and began strutting around the compound showing it off to his grandmother and great-aunt.

I asked Kadek about the *oton* ceremony.

"He is four Bali years old, which means he is almost five by your calendar," she said emphatically. I tried to work it out in my head, but could not. I asked Darta for a pencil and paper. He called to his daughter, who came running from her room with a scrap of paper and a ballpoint pen. Knowing that Adé was actually four years and seven months old, I wrote the following calculation:

The Balinese calendar is 210 days long, so:
4 years and 7 months $= (4 \times 365) + (7 \times 30)$ days
$= 1{,}670$ days
$1{,}670$ days $\div 210$ days $= 8$

So it was actually Adé's eighth *oton*. I realized Kadek's "Bali year" was actually two cycles of the Bali calendar.

The village priest arrived on the back of a motorbike driven by Suda. He was offered a seat up on the Eastern Pavilion and a cup of tea. Abut was sent running out to buy a packet of cigarettes. When Suda, Suti, the two old women, and the priest began discussing the offerings, Suda jumped up and recovered the medium's list from a crook in the roof beams. It had been scratched onto a page torn from a cheap notebook and had since been pored over on many occasions. The five adults stared seriously at what had become little more than a tattered, grubby, little rag. Kadek stayed with Darta, Jean and me. As an office worker and a city girl, her knowledge of offerings was limited. When the conclave broke up, the grandmothers went to work, carrying small offerings into the family temple.

The temple covered an area of about thirteen hundred square feet and took up a little less than a quarter of the entire compound. It was a measure of the Balinese faith that its followers dedicated so much land to their religion. Each of the five shrines within the temple stood about ten feet tall on chest-high carved stone plinths. Two were dedicated to the family ancestors. One of these looked like a little wooden house with three doors and a roof thatched with black sugar-palm fiber. The other had two niches and was made of stone. The household's guardian spirit also had a stone shrine. Offerings to the patron deities of the family members' particular professions or vocations were made at a second wood and thatch shrine. Finally, there was a high throne-like altar in the auspicious northeast corner called a *padmasana*. This shrine was oriented toward the Agung volcano, the abode of the gods. In Darta's words, it functioned "like a telephone. You talk to any deity through that shrine, and they hear you. Also, if you can't make it to some temple ceremony, praying at this shrine will do."

Inside the temple, the grandmothers opened the three small doors of the raised wooden shrine to the family ancestors. They placed offerings both in the shrine and on the stone plinth below. On the Eastern Pavilion, the priest examined the five large, round trays of offerings and the sixth tray with its flowers, pots of water and incense that he would use in his prayers. This last tray also contained a little money for the priest's time. The women moved back and forth between the pavilion and the shrines, showing each tray to the priest and then deploying its contents as instructed.

At first it appeared that the central ritual would take place in the family temple. A mat woven from pandanus leaves was laid out, and on it were placed the priest's tray and the first tray of offerings. After another conversation, however, the whole arrangement was moved out into the center of the compound.

"Ibu misunderstood him," explained Darta.

Final checks were then made on the offerings left in the Eastern

Pavilion. There was considerable discussion over the orientation of a tray containing the eggs and Chinese coins. Both old women offered opinions as to whether the tray should be rotated a few more degrees to the north or to the south. Voices were raised, but consensus emerged, and the ceremony continued.

The priest requested that someone light the incense and went to sit on the mat, facing east toward the temple. It was just before sunset when he purified his hands in the smoke from the incense and held up a first flower in prayer. The air filled with the thick, sweet fragrance of a dozen incense sticks and the sound of mantras being chanted in the archaic Javanese Kawi language. I asked Darta what was going on. He asked me not embarrass him with any further questions about what the priest was saying and asked us to move from the Eastern Pavilion to sit behind the priest. "It's impolite to be in front of him," Darta said.

The Ibus, Kadek, Adé, and his sister, Turia, sat around the priest's mat. Everyone else in the household went about their business as if nothing were going on. The priest sat in the middle of the only route in and out of the house, so people were constantly stepping around him. No one saw any reason to abstain from the usual raucous level of Balinese conversation.

After five minutes, the priest broke from his prayers to tear open the knots in twelve little water-filled plastic bags and pour their contents into a small terra cotta jar. He floated nine petals on the water, sprinkled them with turmeric-yellow rice, and continued his mantras and prayers.

"All the water was collected today from this area," said Darta. "In truth they should have gone to twelve different springs, but that's so difficult. They went to rivers in the north, south, east, and west. Each time they took water they thought of a different spring that fed the river."

Adé had spent long enough posing in his new outfit, and it was time for him to join the proceedings. His shirt and sandals were removed and he was made to stand in the center of a radiating circle of lighted incense sticks laid out on the ground. He had not wanted to enter the circle, and burnt his feet while being pushed in. When the priest sprinkled him with water he recoiled, and burnt himself again.

"He doesn't like to get wet, does he," said Darta.

Adé and Kadek then sat with the priest to pray. While everyone else had their hands raised in prayer, Adé leaned over to wipe his wet hair on his mother's best blouse.

"There's still hope," said Suti. "The ceremony's not over yet."

"The priest always hopes children will be naughty like this," said Darta, "then he can do big ceremonies and make good business."

The priest laid rough-spun strands of cotton on Adé's head and shoulders. Darta explained that this was a special offering, an apology for any mistakes there may have been among the other offerings. Adé got dressed again and followed his mother, grandmother and the priest into the family temple to pray before the ancestral shrine. "From now on it's a normal, simple birthday ceremony," said Darta.

At the end of his prayers, Adé kept asking the priest again and again for more holy water. "I'm thirsty," he said. He got a good pinch on the thigh from his mother for that.

Returning to the Eastern Pavilion, mother, child and priest prayed once more over the remaining offerings. Everyone else sat close by, talking and eating the fruit and cake from the offerings of the first part of the ritual. When the telephone rang somewhere beneath the trays over which the priest was still praying, Darta rummaged around to answer the call. Once the ceremony had been completed, the priest pocketed the five thousand rupiah note from his tray. The old women and Adé's parents thanked him, and he slipped out with Suda before anyone else noticed the event was over.

Later that evening I was sitting on the kitchen floor eating dinner with Wetni, Lolet and Rudy. As in many Balinese households, the family ties between them were distant and convoluted. Rudy was Darta's youngest brother, a bachelor in his late twenties. Lolet was Darta and Rudy's second cousin from Roda's side of the family, and still at school. When Lolet's father died, his mother had dumped her five young children on various relations, then disappeared. Wetni was Ibu's niece and worked as a cook at a local hotel. Her father had been brought to Ubud from their small village for treatment after a serious fall from the top of a coconut tree. A curse on his village said that anyone leaving the community would die. Local interpretation of the curse effectively prohibited the return of those who broke it, since the dead are only supposed to come home in spirit form via the family temple. After Wetni's father's fall, Ibu and Roda had thought he would die anyway without proper treatment and so had moved him to Ubud. A long convalescence and fear of the curse then became the source of a split between Wetni's parents. Since ancestry is traced through the father's side, children are considered to be more their father's than their mother's. Thus Wetni and her older sister, Weti, were brought to Ubud to be taken care of in the household of their aunt. Weti had since moved to Kalimantan, Indonesian Borneo, but Wetni's adoption into the family was so complete that she called her own father Paman, or Uncle.

Half way through our meal, Jean arrived. She had just bathed and looked clean and refreshed. As she stepped up into the kitchen, she stopped and reached to feel her back and shoulders.

"Water," she stated.

"Oh! A *cecak* pissed on you," said Wetni. *Cecak* are small insect-eating lizards that populate the walls and ceilings in Indonesia. "That's very lucky."

"Lucky!" Jean exclaimed.

"Certainly," added Lolet.

Jean got a plate and served herself some food. "I think you're pulling my leg," she said. Ibu wandered into the kitchen just then and Jean told her what had happened.

"How lucky!" Her whole face lit up with the news.

"Think about it, Jean," said Wetni. "How many people are lucky enough to be under a *cecak* when it pisses?" Jean sat down and began to eat. "It could only have been more lucky if it had pissed in your food," Wetni continued. "Bitter. But delicious."

Jean still looked incredulous.

"Jean," said Ibu, "it's because they're holy. They're messengers." If a *cecak* chirps during a contentious conversation, the person who is speaking at the time will often pause, point up at the source of the sound, and then continue with increased confidence, believing the *cecak* has just confirmed the winner of the argument.

Jean nodded her understanding. "But I'm still happy it didn't piss in my food."

Ibu then caught Adé playing with food up on the counter by the stove in the back of the kitchen. Suda came in, grabbed him by an arm, and dragged him down and across the kitchen floor. Rudy grabbed a leg and flicked at Adé's penis through his shorts. Without even offering a whimper of remorse the little escapologist slipped free and ran out into the street.

"Come here! Right here! Right now!" Suda shouted after him. "Do you remember those offerings? Didn't they mean anything to you?" Then he turned to us and said, "He's a little better. But as soon as the ceremony was over, he said that he'd enjoyed it so much and got so many presents that he's going to stay naughty so we have to do it all again."

There being no change in Adé's behavior, the black chick roosting among the lower branches of a tree by the temple was the only remaining sign of the day's activities. Jean and I had thought it would be sacrificed at the ceremony and were surprised to hear it cooing in its sleep. All the ritual paraphernalia had been cleared from the Eastern Pavilion to be replaced by a bamboo table and chairs. Sitting there were Abut and two friends studying for school tests. Suti was talking to them about the *barong* and Rangda. They were enumerating all the rituals required in the making of these sacred masks.

In processions at the beginning and end of temple ceremonies I had often seen Ubud's sacred *barong*. He reminded me of a Chinese New Year dragon, except he was worked by two men, not two dozen. His eyes were wide with surprise. He had snapping jaws, a long, shaggy coat and beard, and his head and tail were decorated with regal gold trappings. He was heavy too, and his carriers were changed every few minutes. In ceremonial performances he frolicked like a puppy. But his sacred power frequently overwhelmed the men who danced him. They often fell into trance.

When Rangda joined the village *barong* in a temple procession, her mask hung on the front of a large basket carried on someone's head. It had horrible fangs, bulging eyes, and a dangling tongue. Knee-length hair was coiled out of sight in the basket. The mask was only worn during temple ceremonies for the occasional midnight trances that ritualize the interplay of good and evil. The full costume included huge, pendulous breasts and long, white fingernails.

One night I saw Rangda attacked with *kris* knives by a dozen men in trance. Had she withdrawn from the stage, her assailants would have turned their knives upon themselves. On this occasion, she stayed. The men knocked her on her back and jumped on her, slamming the points of their *krises* into her chest and belly. She laughed diabolically, immune to the assault. The aura of power surrounding the ceremony was compelling. I was held present by a combination of adrenaline and fear.

The prancing *barong* was required to revive the *kris*-trancers. Each was held down by half a dozen men, touched with the *barong's* beard and sprinkled with holy water. At 4 a.m. Rangda came out once more, this time leading the whole congregation from the temple, down the main street to the burial ground. There she stood in silence with everyone sitting on the ground around her. After twenty minutes, she turned and led us all back to the temple. The closing prayers of the whole village created a remarkable sense of peace.

Jean and I sat on the steps of the Eastern Pavilion listening in on Suti's class. Noticing our interest, she switched the conversation from Balinese to Indonesian, and invited our questions.

"Suti," I said. "What's the difference between sacred *barong* and Rangda masks and the ones that are worn in performances for tourists at the palace?"

"Those used in performances are empty. Only the masks you see up on the altars during temple ceremonies are sacred." Jean and I looked puzzled, so Suti continued. "There is a spirit that lives in a sacred mask. When a carver makes a *barong* or a Rangda he is building that spirit a home. You heard us talking about all the rituals and offerings that must be done. The masks used at the tourist performances are very different. They've never had the *pasupati* animation ceremony."

"Does every village have a *barong* and Rangda?" Jean asked.

"Most villages do. But some communities have a taboo against them."

"They have a taboo against a god?" I was surprised.

"The *barong* isn't really a god. Actually, he's on a level with the animals. He's a servant of Shiva. A village takes care of its *barong* and gives it offerings. In return, the *barong* takes care of the village by scaring away demons with its dance."

"So the *barong* is like a pet, a guard dog!"

"It's not polite to say it that way. But if you do speak like that, then the *barong* would be Shiva's pet, not ours."

"Rangda is a goddess though, isn't she?" said Jean. "She's an aspect of Dewi Durga, and Durga is the wife of Shiva."

"Hmm. How do I explain this? Rangda is the Queen of the Witches, but that doesn't make her a goddess. She is a child of Dewi Durga and is powerful like a goddess. As Durga's representative we treat her like a goddess, but really, she's just a witch. When Rangda leads us all to the cremation ground in the middle of the night, it's so she can visit her mother."

"Is she dangerous? Can she hurt a village?"

"If we befriend her she'll help us."

"You befriend her with offerings, right?"

"Yes. And when she dances, she challenges all the local black-magic practitioners. Witches can't resist her call, but she always defeats them."

At that moment, Darta turned on the television.

"Oh! Oh! Drama!" shouted Abut. He was a big fan of *drama gong*. He loved the gamelan music, the traditional stories and the operatic voices, but most of all he loved the clowns and their ribald jokes. In a flash the school books were packed away. The other children ran for home while Abut installed himself in his father's lap. The whole family gathered to watch the performance.

"Do you want to watch?" I asked Jean.

"Not really," she said. We went back to our porch. Above the crickets and tree frogs we could hear the synchronous laughter of the whole neighborhood.

CHAPTER 8

A Gathering Storm

A week later we met Adé and Kadek on the street. Jean noticed that Adé had broken one of his front upper teeth. It had snapped off right at the gum-line. Just looking at it made my whole mouth ache.

"How on earth did that happen?" asked Jean.

"Sweets," Kadek said. "He was biting on some hard candy."

"Must really hurt."

"Doesn't seem to. It's the third time this has happened. Look next time you see him: another one bottom right, one top left. All from sweets."

I shuddered. "How's he doing since the ceremony?"

"He still has his moments, but we're all noticing that he's a little better."

"But what about Turia?" said Jean. "I met her on the street and she said she'd moved in with your mother to get away from him."

Kadek shook her head. "He makes me so confused, and it makes me sad that Turia can't stay at home with him. When I was her age I'd have given anything to be at home."

Kadek was nearly seven years old when her father died. She, her brother, her two sisters, and her mother then moved from Ubud to Denpasar so her mother could find work. Kadek's mother soon remarried and moved back to Ubud with the younger children, leaving Kadek and her older brother, Putu, with relatives in Denpasar.

"I didn't actually stay with my uncle," recalls Kadek. "I just stayed in a house he owned." The house was rented to a family of Chinese merchants and Kadek became their housekeeper, with her own room and her own entrance. "I swept and cooked for them, and carried a purse full of money for buying groceries and things. I had to get up very early in the morning to get all this done before going to school. The other children made fun of me for always carrying around a big bunch of keys. I told them it was for my house, but nobody believed I was living on my own, not even the teachers. If they had guessed, I'm sure someone from school would have come to check on me." Far from complaining, Kadek recalls it all as something of a dream come true. "I could eat what I wanted, when I wanted, and go where I pleased without anyone stopping me. Now I look at Turia sometimes and shake my head. When I was her age I was doing all this—and she can barely wash her own clothes.

"I didn't come back to Ubud for two years. After that I used to come back only for temple and family ceremonies. In all those years my mother never came to see how I was doing. At the time I didn't think anything of it. I enjoyed the freedom and I didn't know any better. Now I sometimes wonder how she could have just left me like that? But I don't lose any sleep over such things."

Kadek does not often speak about this period in her life. Jean remembers her once talking of a time when she was a street seller, working at the bus terminal, selling newspapers, sweets and cigarettes.

"I was away until junior high school. My brother came back much earlier but, in moving to and from Denpasar, he missed a year of school. There was only one elementary school in Ubud, and if I had come back earlier we would have been in the same class at the same school. My mother said he could never stand that, so I had to stay in Denpasar.

"When Suda was courting me, he didn't believe my stories. He thought I had a vivid imagination. He was very surprised when he asked my mother and she confirmed it was all true."

111

After high school Kadek wanted a career. The only person in a position to help was her uncle in Denpasar, but he wanted her to work for him as a clerk in his shop. Her sights were set higher, so she kept pressing him and he kept refusing. In response to his obstinacy, she ran away. She stayed first with Suda, who was studying Business Administration at a university in Yogyakarta, and then went to Bandung, where she found work. She was away from Bali for nearly a year. When she returned, her uncle finally wrote her a reference. He was either unwilling or unable to continue suppressing such an indomitable spirit.

When she chose to take a career position in the accounting section of the island's water company, it was partly because she could no longer find her place in the offering-making, ceremony-driven economy of village life. Her faith never eroded, but as a street-wise city kid, she had never learned the intricacies of her culture and in some ways had lost the sense of security that lay within those traditions. Her need to work emerged from her experience that she could not depend on others and needed to provide for herself.

"But why feel depressed when it is much better to laugh?" she says. "What happened happened. It happened for many reasons, but that was then, and this is now."

We left Kadek and Adé on the street and walked home. Darta was sitting alone on the steps of the Eastern Pavilion when we arrived. A deep frown creased his brow.

"What's up, Bli?" I asked.

"Confused." He shook his head.

"Confusion seems to be the order of the day," I said. "Kadek's confused because Turia can't stand being with Adé and has moved to her grandmother's."

"I heard," said Darta.

"What's bothering you then?"

"Last night there was a theft in Pujung."

"But that's miles from here."

"A theft from a temple."

"What happened?" said Jean.

"When the symbol for a god is made, whether it be a tiny statue hidden away in a shrine, or a *barong*, or a Rangda mask, there is a very big ceremony that invites the god to animate the symbol. The ceremony involves attaching pieces of silver and gold. These pieces are small, but valuable. Last night someone broke into one of Pujung's temples and stole the symbols, but he didn't get away."

"So?" I said.

"They killed him."

"Killed him!"

"Everyone in the crowd only kicked him once," Darta said defensively. "They didn't mean to."

"So no one knows who he was or where he was from?" asked Jean.

"Only that he was Javaneṣe."

Local temples had been occasionally robbed, mostly to satisfy the desires of Western collectors, but nothing like this had happened in fifteen years.

"People are saying he was from the same group that robbed the store by the market," Darta continued.

"That sounds a bit far-fetched," I said.

"That's what people are saying," Darta repeated.

We all fell into a long silence. Jean broke the spell by changing the subject. "Who's the new girl," she whispered to Darta as a young, pregnant woman crossed from one of the family bedrooms into the kitchen. "I saw her washing up this morning. A cousin?"

"A friend of a friend," said Darta.

"Looks very unhappy."

"She's got good reason to be. She came here for help."

"The father won't marry her?" I asked.

"She's a servant at my friend's house. He's been having a secret affair with her and got her pregnant. Now he wants to take her as his second wife, but he knows that his first wife will be furious if he ever brings it up. As it is she's angry that the girl is so pregnant without the baby's father coming forward to marry her."

Unmarried motherhood is not a concept in the Balinese culture, although premarital pregnancy is not unusual. Even committed partners sometimes wait until the woman gets pregnant before getting married. After marriage the woman moves to her husband's household and performs her religious obeisances at his family shrines. Without a father and his family temple, both child and mother are without roots. They become homeless. In a culture where most social events are also ceremonial, they are unable to enter any temple, and are effectively banished by their community.

"So your friend brought her here?"

"No. One of his friends did."

"Is that who you were having coffee with this morning?"

"Right."

Locally, Darta has the reputation for being a font of good counsel. Due to his legal background, people come to him for advice. In this case he also had another friend from elementary school whom everyone thought could help.

"I wouldn't have said he was my friend," protested Darta. "We were just in the same class. He was a very strange child. He used to ride his bicycle without ever using the brakes. He'd shoot straight out into the traffic." Darta mimed near-accidents with his hands. "To stop himself he would ride into piles of sand. At school he chewed the sharp corner of his desk until it was quite round, then he started down the leg. He used to eat whole pens and pencils. I always kept mine very close, in my pocket. I never left anything lying around for him to eat. One day he asked me for my shirt and I gave it to him. Otherwise he would have hit me and knocked me down. He failed a year at school and had to redo it, then he dropped out and I didn't think about him for a long time. When I heard about him again, they said he was meditating in temples and visiting the river at night. People were saying he might have become a magician. So I went to see for myself. There were three car parks full of cars near his house and many people waiting to see him. He really had become a magician!

"So my friend wanted me to take this girl to him to make her miscarry. We went there and my old classmate took some holy water, said some mantras over it, and gave it to the girl. 'Don't drink it now,' he said, 'or you'll miscarry too early in the morning. Wait until morning and it will happen twelve hours later.' So the next day she drank the water, but nothing happened. Now they're looking for someone to take her as a second wife and give the child a home."

On another occasion Darta was approached to mediate a similar situation. A girl at a nearby homestay was pregnant, but without a potential husband. A compromise was arranged whereby someone was paid to marry the girl, but was then free to leave. Thus the child was fathered and neither mother nor baby were considered ritually impure. Five years later the jury-rigged solution was straining at the seams. The child, a boy, would have had rights to his step-father's lands, had not those rights been signed away before the arranged marriage. Therefore, when the boy himself married, he would have nowhere to take his bride. Somehow, as matchmaker, Darta was being regarded by those concerned as the father in terms of an inheritance for the boy.

"But that's another problem entirely," said Darta philosophically.

A week later we were walking back from the crossroads toward the family house when Rudy almost ran us over with his moped. He stopped to apologize and said he was upset. We asked why?

"The sacred *barong* in Tegalalang has had its beard cut off. It was done last night, but no one was seen coming or going from the temple. Then this morning the village head received a typewritten letter."

"What did it say?" I asked.

Rudy took a deep breath. "It said, 'You have killed one of us but there are many more to follow. We are sixty and we have vowed to destroy the Hindu religion. By reputation the Balinese people are fierce in defense of their land and their beliefs, but how strong will they really prove to be?' It was written in Indonesian, not Balinese."

"Was it signed? Did it give the name of the group?"

"No. It was just a message."

Ubud's response was immediate. The people were incensed.

Two temple attacks and the theft in the marketplace had the whole town up in arms. Nighttime guard duty was set up in the village temples. Venturing into town after dark meant running the gauntlet through bands of men who shone flashlights in your face and brandished long coconut-wood truncheons. The patrols wore black-and-white hip cloths to symbolize their roles as peacekeepers, but their attitude was anything but defensive. Local Javanese were warned to stay in at night: their safety could not otherwise be guaranteed. Tourists felt unsafe and began leaving in droves for other parts of the island. The village considered the financial implications insignificant compared to the threat voiced in the letter.

Rumor connected the whole series of events to the upcoming ceremony at the new temple on Mount Semeru in Java. Reports of ten to twenty thousand local Hindu converts in East Java, plus the fact that much of the money for the temple had come from Ubud, were thought to have fueled an Islamic fundamentalist backlash.

The streets became wilder every night. We overheard Ibu comparing it to the atmosphere of violence that followed the attempted coup d'état in October, 1965. Bali had been one of the areas worst hit by the blood bath. Few Balinese ever speak of what happened, and we had never heard Ibu mention the killings before.

"Doesn't this frighten you?" I asked Jean.

"I'm frightened, but not of immediate violence. It's like walking the streets of a bad neighborhood back home. There is the potential for violence. I keep looking over my shoulder. I watch people with suspicion."

"Who'd have thought we'd feel this in Bali?"

"I don't feel they're about to beat me, though. My skin's the wrong color for that. Mostly, I'm shocked by how angry their smiling faces have become."

Ubud lost several hundred lives to the bloodletting that followed the attempted coup in late 1965. There are no official statistics to quote, but Darta remembers seeing men he knew ride by in the back of trucks at the end of March, 1966. They were driven three miles north to Petulu and shot dead.

Several thousand white herons now roost in the trees of Petulu village. The birds fly home every evening over Ubud. Some people recall loved ones in the passing of a long formation of birds against a slate-gray sky. Others must remember killing neighbors. Certainly, a few have hardened their hearts against such memories. Whatever the personal response, by unspoken consensus, the birds remain the only, poignant reminder.

Jean and I sat on our back porch as a flight of herons wafted silently overhead. The tension on the streets continued, and it began to wear on us.

"It somewhat shatters a dream doesn't it," I said. "Paradise falling apart around our ears."

"This isn't supposed to be happening," said Jean. "They always said they had learned their lesson from those times."

"Perhaps they did. But they're not the ones out on the streets every night. Have you noticed who's in those gangs? It's Rudy and his peers. They were babes-in-arms in 1966. They don't remember what happened then and they've got nothing better to do now. Their families are well off, so they don't have to work like their parents did. The work used to be shared equally, the women at home and the men in the fields. It's still that way for most of Bali. But things have changed here. The men now work with the tourists, and that's seasonal work at best. The young ones especially are bored, and unspent testosterone and religious fervor are a volatile combination." I sighed. "For a few moments, being with the family in Java and in the comfort of our first days back here, I really felt a sense of belonging. I thought we might just choose to stay here."

"You never told me that."

"I didn't quite believe it. How would we make a living? What would we do?"

"And what's going on has changed your mind about living here?"

"Hasn't it changed yours?"

"I never thought of staying," said Jean. "I thought we were here while we figured out where to go next. But they haven't run amok yet, and I still say this is less violent than the streets of America. If I've learnt anything from these people it's that you hang in there with those you love."

"But it leaves me feeling empty. We were so busy getting ready to leave Tokyo and it was so much fun being on the road again that I never really had the time to think about where we were going. We came here because it's always provided answers. What kind of answer is this? Right now I'm afraid to go out at night. We didn't even need to lock the front door of our little house in Japan."

"You regretting that we left?"

"No. It was time to leave. But we left in search of community. I'd always held up this place as such a healthy model. I wanted to learn things that would help us wherever we ended up. Lynch mobs aren't anything I have an interest in."

"So what you've seen and heard has undermined how you feel about Darta and Suti and Pung and Ibu?"

"Of course not."

"Does it make sense to you? This holy war thing? Do you believe it?"

"There was a letter."

"It said sixty people. It might be just one crazy."

"The villagers had already killed one when the letter was written, so there are at least two."

"People take advantage of situations like this. The theft, the desecration of the *barong*, the letter; those responsible could be completely unconnected except by a desire to fan the flames. Look. I've seen Rudy lose his temper and throw every pot, pan, plate, glass, cup, knife, fork, and spoon out of the kitchen into the garden. He went berserk! Everyone else just sat around and watched. It was hilarious. When he had finished, they swept up what was broken and put the rest back in the cupboards. I've seen Darta drag the wardrobe out of his bedroom and smash it to pieces. He was so embarrassed afterward. My point is they can be quick to temper, but it doesn't always mean very much."

"But now they're killing people!"

"I know. I'm just asking you not to get swept away by all their emotion. They are volatile, you're right. But be far enough from the fire so that you don't get burned, too. If the deaths worry you, start getting upset about all the deaths that happen everyday on the roads here from the bad driving. It's not easy here right now, but put it into perspective." Jean poured me a glass of water. "William, let's get away for a while. We'll go down to the beach. This'll all have cooled off in a few days."

"Sure. Why not," I said.

CHAPTER 9

Eclipsed

It was a pleasant surprise to see Pung walking up the garden path with breakfast the next morning. "Just like old times," I said. He very seriously served us our breakfast. "Pung. You're as stiff as an English butler this morning! What's gotten into you?"

He rolled his eyes, put down his tray, sat on the porch between us, and began talking in a low and very precise voice about his upcoming *oton* birthday. "Very secret," he kept saying in English as we ate.

That Pung had a secret was surprising all by itself. In a Balinese home there are few places to hide personal possessions and fewer opportunities for privacy. Pung might be keeping a secret from a specific person, but this would only be possible with the collaboration of those he lived with.

I got the impression that we were Pung's only confidants in the matter of his *oton*. But this didn't make sense. Why was the date of his birthday a secret? Anyone with the inclination could look it up on a calendar. I got up and went into our room to do exactly that. The calendar hung on the back of the door.

"My next *oton* is on *Kajeng-Kliwon* and the full moon," said Pung. The *oton* is the birthday that occurs once in every two-hundred-and-ten-day Balinese year. *Kajeng-Kliwon* comes around every fifteen days, when a great number of offerings are required to appease the day's disruptive spirits. Full moon is an equally powerful though auspicious day requiring another outpouring of offerings. "This happened to me once before, in my first year of junior high school, and my mother made a big ceremony for me." The conjunction is only supposed to happen for temple ceremonies when gods have their birthdays. Accordingly, it is frighteningly auspicious for a mere mortal.

I came out of our room holding a Balinese-Gregorian calendar. Its dual function served both ceremonial and mercantile interests. "*Kajeng-Kliwon*—that's next Saturday," I said. "But full moon—it says here that full moon is next Friday, Pung. And there's a total eclipse as well. Jean, there's a lunar eclipse next week, eight in the evening till just after midnight, according to this." I turned to Pung again. "So, when's your birthday? *Kajeng-Kliwon* or full moon?"

"You see," began Pung, "my birthday is on *Tumpek-Wayang*, which is also *Saniscara-Wayang*, the seventh day of the twenty-seventh seven-day week. This day always falls on *Kajeng-Kliwon*, which is when the third day of the three-day week and the fifth day of the five-day week coincide. On your calendar, that's always a Saturday. But *Tumpek-Wayang*-full-moon-total-eclipse is very rare!" We both nodded stupidly. Pung loved to confuse us. "You see why my birthday is so secret?"

We both shook our heads. "Well, no," I said. "But we're very honored that you've told us about it."

It was Pung's turn to look puzzled. "What do you mean?"

"Well, what are you telling us for if it's secret?" said Jean.

"No! It's not a secret. It's secret!"

"We know, you keep telling us," I said.

"Ah-do!" We were straining his patience. "Secret! Like religious."

"Oh! You mean sacred!" said Jean.

"Sacred! Yes, sacred. Why is my mouth so stupid?"

"Pung!" Jean and I both said at once. He was always much too self-deprecating about his English.

"Do you know why it's sacred?" he asked.

"We barely know why it is at all," said Jean.

"*Tumpek-Wayang*," began Pung, "is a very special day for *dalangs*, like my great-uncle, Pekak Dalang." A *dalang* is a shadow puppeteer. "He will take out all of his puppet shadows." Pung

121

often made the endearing mistake of confusing puppet shadows with shadow puppets. "Then he will set them up for a performance, and do a special blessing. It is a good day for the puppet shadows, but a very, very unlucky day to be born on. The bad luck can be made into good luck, though. My family always has to do a special ceremony to purify me and keep me safe. Pekak Dalang must always do a daytime performance for me, and the puppet Tualèn must always speak to the gods for me."

"But what about this day and full moon being on different days?" I asked.

"They're not."

"Look at the calendar."

"Yes, but it depends. Some people celebrate the day before and some people the day after the night of the full moon. Also our lunar calendar says the full and new moons are every fifteen days. But that doesn't work. Full moon to full moon isn't thirty days. Look at the calendar again, Bli. Every nine Wednesdays there is a double-day as a correction."

"So your birthday is always *Tumpek-Wayang*," I stated.

"Yes."

"And this year it's also a full moon and an eclipse."

"Yes. I'll have to go home for this. It'll be a big ceremony."

"Should we come to your party?" Jean asked.

"Lots of offerings. Lots of sitting around. Not much ceremony. Better you stay here and watch the eclipse by yourself."

"Pung, I have a question," said Jean. "But maybe it'll make you shy." She had been talking to me about Pung's relationship with Wetni since we woke up. I knew she had been eager to talk to Pung about it, too.

"No really, it's not such a big ceremony. We can easily afford it." Pung had misunderstood and Jean's moment passed. We started talking about the motorbike his father had bought him. Though not a man of means, Pung's father was proud of his son's work with the tourists in Ubud and had gone into debt buying him what he saw as the appropriate transportation. The bike had made Pung quite the star in his small village. Then his father started having trouble making the payments and wanted to sell land rather than the bike. Pung then took the stiff payments on himself.

"All the money I earn as a guide or driver goes to the bank," he said. "But that's OK. I don't smoke. I don't drink. I have a roof over my head living with Suda. All I need is food. There's four hundred thousand rupiah left to pay. When that's done I'll sell the bike, move back to my village and build myself a house."

"Who with?" injected Jean. We were back on her subject. Pung would not be moving home alone. He almost blushed, but said nothing. "Pung," Jean continued. "Are you and Wetni like brother and sister? Or is it possible that you might get married?"

"I've known Wetni since 1985," began Pung. "That's eight years. A long time." He was not at all embarrassed to talk. "We worked together at the café and lived together here. We talk a lot. She is very good to me."

"I remember," said Jean. "Every time Wetni and I talked about your mom she would cry and say, 'It makes me so sad. I can't talk about Pung's mom without crying.'"

"Wetni and I have always been able to talk about things from the heart." Pung was speaking very softly. "We are very close. She understands what I'm feeling." He begun weeping. "She helped me a lot when my mother died." He wiped the back of his hand across his eyes. "There are other girls up in my home village who want to marry me. But I think they want me because they think I have money. I'm very shy around them. It's a strange feeling. I have had a lot of girlfriends, but none of them have been right with my heart like Wet is."

Jean said, "I know a lot of people get married to have children or to make a home. But I married William beacuse he's my best friend. Like Suti and Darta, I think they can talk about anything."

Pung nodded.

"Do you know how Wetni feels?"

"Yes. I know." Pung was just staring at the floor.

"In my dreams I often see you and Wetni married. I'd love it if you two were married." Tears ran down Jean's face, too. "That'd be great." Pung was all choked up. He couldn't say anything more. He just patted Jean on the knee, got up and walked back towards the kitchen.

"I knew it!" said Jean through her tears. "Love-struck!"

"What made you think anything was going on?"

"Wetni's got a new ring. I asked her where she got it. She said Pung gave it to her, and that it was his mother's."

Less than a year after Jean first arrived in Bali, Pung came to her and said, "Can you take me to see my mother. She has very bad rheumatism."

Pung was sixteen and local transportation was such that traveling home to his village was a long, arduous task. His mother was visiting relatives in Denpasar and seeing a famous healer in the city. This was a good opportunity for Pung to see his family. Jean had recently bought the white van and was still its only driver.

Pung's mother was already in a lot of pain when Jean first saw her. Her legs were terribly swollen, from hip to foot. She let Jean examine her, but wasn't able to chit-chat. The condition was obviously more serious than rheumatism, so Jean suggested they take her to the public hospital for some blood tests. After leaving Pung's parents at the Emergency Room, Pung and Jean went home.

They didn't return to Denpasar for two days due to a ceremony in Ubud. When they went back to the hospital, Darta came along to help communicate with the doctor. Pung went to see his mother while Jean and Darta went straight to the doctor's office. He told them that Pung's mother had leukemia and suggested they send her immediately to Jakarta for chemotherapy and a bone marrow transplant. "They have the hermetically-sealed wards required for recovery from such a treatment there," he said. Jean remembers thinking that the existence of a truly hermetically-sealed room in Indonesia was unlikely. "If you want better treatment, you could send her to Singapore," the doctor continued.

"She's going to die, isn't she?" asked Jean.

"Yes," the doctor replied.

"I can't afford to send her to Jakarta or Singapore, and anyway, it would be a waste of money, wouldn't it?"

"Yes."

"So there's no point in treating her. Just make her comfortable."

The doctor agreed there should be no treatment. He would simply try to ease her pain.

"Do you have morphine?" Jean asked.

The doctor nodded his consent. "She will soon be in a lot of pain. We will give her painkillers and blood transfusions to keep her energy up."

"No blood transfusions," said Jean. "You'll take the blood from her family, won't you? They can't afford to give blood. And it's pointless. It won't really help her and it will give them a false sense of hope."

Darta and Jean then went down to the ward. There were rats running around everywhere. Two patients had died in the night and were still lying in their beds. Pung, his father and his older brothers were crowded around the end of Pung's mother's bed, just watching her. The swelling had spread to her neck. She was semi-conscious and moaned constantly. Jean ordered the hospital to move her immediately to a private room, though Pung's father thought it was a waste of money. Jean, Darta and Pung then went back to Ubud.

They returned the next afternoon. Ashen family members were lying all along the corridor when they arrived. All had their arms bandaged where they had given blood. Inside the room, Pung's father was pale but smiling. "She'll get better now, won't she?" he said. Pung's mother was drifting in and out of consciousness. Her neck was huge and her breasts were impossibly distended. Pung just sat on the end of her bed with his back to her. Being physically close was as intimate as any of the family members got with one another. They didn't touch. Jean sat with Pung's mother, stroking her hand.

At home that night, Jean talked to Darta. "The doctors haven't told any of them, have they?"

"No. They told you, and thought that would be enough."

"But I'm not family. I'm just the foreigner paying the bills!"

"When Roda was dying, he wanted to know, so he could help his family get ready. But not everyone is that strong. Usually the family knows, but the sick person isn't told so that he or she doesn't lose hope."

"But they haven't even told the family," Jean said.

"They told us."

"So we have to tell them?"

Darta nodded. "I think so."

Jean walked over to the café to talk to Pung. It was near closing time. She found him in the kitchen with Wetni.

"Pung, I have to tell you about your mother's illness." Pung was biting his lip, but looked her straight in the eye. "It's very bad. She has cancer and there isn't going to be a cure. I'm so sorry, Pung."

"He didn't say anything," Jean recalls. "He just walked past me out into the night. I just stood there, with Wetni crying in the corner. He came back much later. 'We should take her home,' was all he said.

"At the hospital the next day Darta told the family. I waited out in the corridor. For a long time there was just Darta's voice. Then Pung's father started screaming. I went in, and he was pulling at his hair, pounding his head on the wall. His knees kept giving way and he would fall to the floor, then try to stand again. He went on like this for hours. The other family members, Pung's brothers, were silent, just staring. I don't think Pung's mother was conscious of any of this. She was even more bloated than the day before, and very quiet.

"Then the nurses started pushing bills under my nose. I had to pay for all the transfusions I had expressly requested they avoid, and there were bills for drugs, too. Before paying, I demanded to see her charts. I wanted to see what they had really been doing. They didn't want to show me, but I was insistent. They took me to the ward office, and I looked at her chart. All they'd been giving her was Valium. I went ballistic. I threw the chart across the office and stormed back to the room to find a whole pack of trainee doctors examining her. They had her shirt lifted up and they were poking her breasts. I shouted at them, threw them all out, and demanded to see the doctor. He wasn't available, so I went to sit in his office. I waited two hours, and when he came, he had nothing to say to me. I told him we were taking her home. Back in the hospital room I sat on the bed, holding her hand, and told everyone I thought we should take her home. I remember she turned her head toward me then and looked right at me. There was no emotion left to read in her face, but I felt she was saying, yes, she wanted to go home. Then she turned away again. The family agreed to move her and went to get a car.

"We took the seats out of the hired minibus and stuffed them in the white van. We carefully carried Pung's mother out of the hospital on a stretcher and lay her in the back, on the metal floor, on a single blanket. Everyone else squashed into the van and we drove for three hours to the village. She didn't make a sound during the whole trip. When we reached the end of the road there were about forty-five or fifty men waiting to carry her the twenty minutes into the village. One of the brothers had returned by motorbike to find help. You know how Balinese are usually all chatter? These men were just squatting, in complete silence, by the side of the road. It was sunset. The sky was blood red. They just put her across their shoulders and carried her away. No one said a word. Pung went with them. I went home with Darta.

"Three days later, Pung came back to Ubud to say that his mother had died, and that he would be away for a few days more. His mother was to receive a special cremation as soon as possible. When she married Pung's father, who is one of the village priests, she was automatically ordained. There are no high priests of the Brahmana caste in the area of their village, so the village priests perform the more sacred ceremonies, such as cremations, usually reserved for the Brahmana priests. This meant that Pung's mother needed a cremation worthy of a high priest. When Pung told me this, he didn't ask me for money. He just told me she would have to be cremated at the next auspicious opportunity, in just three more days. They had already started preparations, but needed to buy offerings from outside the village to finish all the elaborate work in time. Pung told me that his father was going to sell all his rice fields to get the money he needed. They were also borrowing the equivalent of two hundred and fifty dollars from the village. Pung said, 'My father can't think properly. He's confused about what to do.' I asked how much money they were short. He told me they needed just over a thousand dollars. We went up together the next day by motorbike. I had the money in my pocket.

"I was there for just two nights. That night and the night before the cremation. Pung said I had to come, but at that time I didn't know anybody there. Pung took me around the village, and briefly introduced me to everyone. But there were too many people to remember.

"I can't really tell you in what order everything happened, you'll have to ask Pung if you want to know that. But I do remember their grief. It was overwhelming. Pung's mother died at the age of forty-two. She was the mother of nine—five boys, four girls. The youngest was about five at the time. People told me how, even when she had very little food, she would share it with any of the village children who were around the house. She must have been a lot like Suti that way. And she was so suddenly gone. Pung's father was still taking it badly. He just sat on his porch.

"It wasn't all pain and anguish though. There were so many offerings to make—even though they'd bought the more complicated ones. Half the village was there to help. People were talking and laughing while they worked, just like usual. They all found it very funny that I couldn't make even the simplest offering, no matter how many times they showed me.

"I remember Pung's grandfather, his mother's father, coming into the compound in the evening. He just stood behind me, with his hands on my shoulders, his wiry old fingers squeezing into me. He had loved his daughter so much, I hear he's never been able to visit that house again since the cremation. We didn't know it at the time, but while their daughter was sick, he and Pung's grandmother had been to the Temple of the Dead, where they were the priests. They did something very dangerous. They made a special offering at the shrine to the Goddess Durga asking her to take them and spare their daughter.

"After the death, the body lay in the pavilion in the center of the compound. It didn't smell, except mildly of some chemicals. I think they must have drained it and injected something. Before the cremation, all the brothers helped wash her body. She was naked, and they held her up, washing and anointing her all over with oils and flowers. It was very beautiful. I was right up there with them. Pung asked me to photograph everything. I was so glad to have that camera. It kept me at a distance from all that was going on.

"After the washing, they wrapped her in a long, white cloth that draped down onto the ground, like an umbilical cord. On the night before a cremation, everyone has to stay up all night to guard the body against bad spirits. As always, there was a noisy group of gamblers up on the pavilion. Pung was right beside them, sitting on the floor, hugging the white cloth as it draped over his shoulder. He just sat there silently with his legs crossed, rocking back and forth, holding onto that cloth.

"Despite all this pain, Pung knew exactly what to do. He was constantly giving directions through all those preparations. He knew everything that had to be done—people said that was unusual for someone of his age. Maybe it was because he had seen it so many times before, but I was still in awe.

"The morning of a cremation is always full of socializing and sitting around. The whole village was there. Pung's grandfather officiated. They carried the body out and put it in the big gold and white tower they had built to carry the body to the cremation ground. Thirty men carried the tower, led by a long piece of white cloth which family members carried overhead. Everyone marched through the village accompanied by a gamelan orchestra. Pung and his oldest brother, Wayan, rode with their mother up on the tower. At the cremation ground, they took the body from the tower and lay it on a simple bamboo and banana-stem pyre with a whole pile of offerings. Then they doused it all with kerosene and burned it to ash. I kept taking pictures and thinking about the thousand dollars that were going up in smoke. Only a few villagers stayed to witness the fire. No one is supposed to cry at a cremation or within sight of the body because they might cause the soul of the deceased to be doubtful about moving on.

"The ceremonies went on through the early hours of the next morning. The ashes from the first cremation were released into a nearby river. Then they started getting ready for the night's second cremation during which an effigy was burned to finally release Pung's mother's soul from this world. Other places in Bali don't perform this second ritual so quickly. I felt too exhausted, physically and emotionally, to stay up and keep photographing. Actually, Darta turned up that evening in the family car to save me. My knight and his white charger. I was so glad to see him. I talked his ear off all the way home. I just had to share what I'd seen with someone.

"What most impressed me was how fully everyone expressed their grief, and also how little physical support people gave to one another. Darta said it was because they were mountain folk. He said his family had all hugged Roda's body and hugged each other and wailed and cried terribly.

"Sometimes when Pung and I are in Denpasar, buying something for the family or whatever, he bargains for both of us. He tells the seller, 'This isn't a tourist. She's my family. Treat her like any other Balinese. Give her a good price.' The seller says that we're like mother and son, and we laugh. But it's happened more than once. Even though we weren't able to talk much through those horrible weeks, a bond was created between us. And that will never be undone."

The morning after the conversation with Pung about Wetni, we left for the beach. We packed a light bag of clothes and a heavy one full of books and set out to catch the midday tourist shuttle to Candi Dasa beach.

"Ibu, Suti," Jean called on our way through the front of the house. "Keep the room. We'll be back in a few days, in time for the full moon. And get ready for a party. You all need a party. There's too much tension around here. We're going to take you all up into the rice fields to watch the eclipse!"

Five nights later we were sitting in the dark, with the whole family, on a path through the paddies. "I must be going crazy," muttered Ibu, "sitting up here in the dead of night." The old woman could hardly believe what she was doing. The world may appear to belong to man by day, but after nightfall ghosts and spirits of every kind take over, traveling the same ways and using the same small rice field paths.

"Ibu," said Rudy. "We're making much too much noise for anything to come and disturb us. Look at the moon. It's beautiful."

"It's just the moon. Looks the same to me as it does every month at this time."

"Just wait. It'll start any minute."

Ibu, Rudy, Darta, Suti, Suda, Kadek, all the children, Jean and I lounged around on a few mats beneath the clear and starry skies. We were among the paddies along the path just above the family house. Nearby was a temple dedicated to the rice goddess Dewi Sri. Such temples are the ceremonial hubs of each rice-growing community. Behind us was the little six-foot-square meeting pavilion to which Jean and I had often come to watch the sunset when we were first in Bali together.

After only twenty minutes, almost everybody had neck-aches from looking up at the moon. Darta had brought his pillow and laid himself out with his head propped up at the appropriate angle. He tapped me on the back, and when I turned toward him he nodded heavenwards. One by one we all turned to look. The top right-hand edge of the full moon was touched by the merest velvet hint of darkness. If I kept my sights fixed on a certain point on the moon's surface, I could see the flowing movement of the earth's shadow across the moon's seas and islands of rock and sand. From a number of different corners of the surrounding night came the sounds of people banging on pots, pans and dustbins. "Kids," explained Darta. The banging on pots and pans was for earthquakes, to wake up the serpents Basuki and Anantaboga when they fell asleep on the job of holding the earth's foundations together, and to scare off Kala Rahu during a lunar or solar eclipse when he tried to eat the moon or the sun. "When the demon Kala Rahu stole the Water of Immortality from the gods, the sun and moon saw him. When they told Vishnu, he sent a lightning bolt to cut off Kala Rahu's head. Kala Rahu was just about to drink the water when he was cut in two. He had the water in his mouth. So his head became immortal and his body died. Now he chases the sun and moon, and when he catches them, he eats them. But he has no body and when he swallows they come out again and get away. We bang on pots to scare the demon away during a solar eclipse, but don't often bang on things for a lunar eclipse. No one could keep going that long." The children in one nearby village seemed to be having a go, however.

"You do your culture an injustice," I said, thinking of the

considerable stamina the Balinese have when it comes to making noise. They are never quiet, except in prayer, and talk all the way through even their most favorite drama performances. They were talking and laughing now, looking every which way but at the moon. When I noticed that Jean had become quiet, I followed her lead. In our silence we echoed each other's sense of wonder.

A solar eclipse is sudden and violent, robbing light from the day and sight from those who look directly at it. A lunar eclipse is slow, mellow and watery. It gives you time to think: A moon, spinning around an aqueous world; the world, wheeling about a fiery sun; the sun, a minor participant within the spiral arms of a huge galaxy; the galaxy, seen as a milky wash across the night; and the world's shadow, thrown upward toward the Milky Way by the sun, seen only when the moon offers itself as a screen for this most understated of cosmic shadow plays. Beings sitting on a small island somewhere near the planet's equator are infinitesimally small on the scale of such an event, but also inescapably bound into the nexus of its happening.

Just as the old woman said, the moon was the same as it had always been: size and spin perfectly matched to the period of its rotation around the world, always presenting the same magically improbable face to the world-bound onlooker. The cosmic drama was moving in the same way as it does every night. The twisting galaxy, the shining star, the spinning moon and planet were not shifting in their roles. This was merely a passing revelation of an underlying conspiracy, the deepest of nature's secrets briefly visible in a blood-red shadow.

As the minutes passed, and the family children and then the adults grew bored with the spectacle, it became increasingly difficult to remain focused in our sense of awe. When Turia presented me with a small banana-leaf boat of *kolak*, a cocktail of banana, sweet potato and pineapple in coconut milk with palm sugar, it was hard to refuse. I became earthbound once more. She handed me an elegant little palm-leaf spoon, and I thanked her.

"Who made this?" I said.

"Suti," said Ibu.

"There's plenty. Eat as much as you want," said the chef.

Ibu had carried a huge jar of water on her head for the party.

Tutut had brought a basket full of cups and glasses. "Here," Ibu said, handing me a brimming glassful.

Sipping my water, I turned back to the moon. It was so beautiful. I was in awe. Why wasn't the family?

Jean and I had once sat with Suda beside the Ayung river in one of the most picturesque gorges on the island. When we said how beautiful it was he laughed. "As a child I used to come to this river to visit a friend. We slept at night in his hut and woke up at first light. It was the most ordinary place I could think of. I was young and strong and barely noticed how steep the valley was. But we played all day, and that made me very happy. When you say this is beautiful, I hear what you say, but I really don't understand what you mean."

An old Chinese proverb that I once copied into my journal says:

> If there is light in the soul,
> There will be beauty in the person.
> If there is beauty in the person,
> There will be harmony in the house.
> If there is harmony in the house,
> There will be order in the nation.
> If there is order in the nation,
> There will be peace in the world.

Our attraction to Bali had always been to the light in the soul of each Balinese. After our day on the river with Suda I wondered if, with light in the soul and beauty in the person, there would be any calling to take note of beauty in the world. The mind's attention is always drawn most strongly to contrast, but if one has a sense of inner-beauty, there is no gradient to observe. Only when the inner and outer worlds fall into sharp discord does something call out to us. "This place is so beautiful" could equally be stated in the converse: "I feel so ugly." The more Jean and I talked about this, the clearer it seemed. So many people, ourselves included, come to Bali in search of beauty and in reaction to some dark feeling of emptiness within ourselves. We come with minds full of questions and pockets full of money hoping to appropriate, by straightforward purchase or a more subtle osmosis, some small quantum of light to illuminate the gaping space within. We come with a desperate need for some of their light to touch us. The two-fold miracle is not only that it does, but that they so willingly give their light away.

As the moon continued along its hour-long arc into the full shade of the earth, Darta began giving us news of what we had missed while at the beach.

"Na. The day after you left, everyone was crazy again. We heard that someone had cut the hair of the *barong* in Sebali. People were out on the street questioning anything that moved. Before I joined in, I wanted to see for myself what had happened in Sebali. It's only a few kilometers away, north of Campuhan. So about half a dozen of us walked up there and asked to see the damaged mask. When we got there, nobody knew what we were talking about. The village almost panicked. People ran to check the *barong*, thinking we were bringing news that he had been damaged!

"Na. A village *barong* is often given the name Ratu Gedé. And the word for leather in Balinese is *blulang*. The news from Sebali said, '*Ratu Gedé blulangina,*' which is ambiguous. It means both 'the *barong* is cut from leather' and 'the *barong's* leather is cut.' The first meaning is obvious. Whoever first told the story wanted it to be taken the other way." Darta laughed. He loved laughing at his own stories, and his laughter was infectious.

"Someone with nothing better to do was playing games," growled Suda. His immunity to Darta's jokes is mostly a matter of theater. Every comic needs a straight man. "This is like that farmer and his snake over in Gianyar."

"Ah! That snake." Having planted the seed of the next story, Suda let his brother continue. "Just off the main road between here and Gianyar, a farmer had a rice-field terrace with a big cave in its wall. A rumor began that the farmer had seen a huge python in the cave, and many, many people went there to get a look." We knew that big pythons around Ubud were no flight of fancy. A Westerner with a house above a forested valley had recently stumbled into her kitchen in the middle of the night to discover a huge snake eating her cat. "The farmer dried out some of his fields and opened them as a parking lot, with a fee. Sellers paid him for the right to set up food stands. Special charter buses were arranged; whole villages came to see. I even went! I went two or three times and never saw the snake, nor did I meet anyone there who had ever seen the snake. Even the owner of the land, when asked, kept saying, 'As long as I've lived, I've never seen such a snake!' And I don't think he was lying. It was true, he never had seen such a snake."

"*Bogbog*, Bli!" said Rudy. *Bogbog* means tall tale in Balinese.

Darta huffed indignantly. Suti came to his rescue. "It's true. I remember the stories."

The moon had been hanging scarlet and apparently static for at least half an hour. We tried to entertain the children, pointing out the pattern of craters and seas across the moon's surface that the Japanese see as a rabbit with long ears pounding rice with a huge mallet in an equally large mortar. They were unimpressed. It was time to pull the ace out of our little party hat. The *kolak* had been given time to digest. It was time for the chocolate cake we had bought from one of the tourist restaurants in town. Adé chose to wear more of his piece than he ate. Abut, Tutut and Turia were a little more reserved. The remaining slices were cut in half and served to the adults.

Just then a middle-aged man Ibu obviously knew came wandering by out of the dark. "Where are you going, out here, at this time of the night?" she demanded.

The man, in a torn T-shirt and dirty sarong, was startled by the challenge. "Water. I was just checking the water in my fields," he said defensively.

"How do we know you have paddies out here." Darta took up the game. "You could be anyone coming into the village at this time of the night. It's a good thing we caught you. Who knows what you might have done!"

"But *Pan* Abut, it's me!" the man protested. Like many Balinese men, Darta was usually addressed using his son's name. Even his wife called him Father of Abut.

"He knows your name!" exclaimed Rudy.

"Lucky guess," said Darta.

"Lucky guess! What do you mean? We went to school together!" said the man. "Hey!" He finally saw what was before his eyes. "What on earth are you all doing up here?"

"We're watching the eclipse and eating chocolate cake," said Ibu. "We've all gone completely crazy. Here, sit down and join us. Someone give him a piece of cake."

The man sat down. Nobody introduced him, but then no one but us needed the introduction. "You shouldn't scare a man like that," he said. "Not after what I just heard."

Now he had everyone's attention. "What did you hear?" pressed Suda.

"Up near Klabang Moding, Gusti Aji was mistaken for a thief. If one of his friends hadn't been in the crowd, shouting up for him, he'd be dead."

Darta, ever mindful of our presence, translated the colloquial Balinese and explained that Gusti Aji was the head of the rice-growing community to the west of where we sat. His business often took him northward, up the watershed, to refine the flow of irrigation waters over weirs and through sluices, to look for leaks, and to optimize the amount of water coming onto his community's land.

"How is he?" asked Ibu.

"A bit battered and bruised, but he'll survive."

The news provided a break in the festive atmosphere which the children exploited with calls to return home. Ibu agreed that enough was enough and asked for help gathering up the picnic things. The family left, leaving only Suda and Darta to stay with us in the dark.

"How much longer will this eclipse last?" asked Suda.

"Another couple of hours," I said.

"Stress. Too much stress," he said.

"Watching the moon?"

"No!" He slapped playfully at my arm. "Whoever is making all of these problems. Yes, it started in Pujung. But then it was Tegalalang. And next the story about Sebali—which turned out to be a play on words. A play on words in Balinese—I don't think that was a Javanese group. I think the people who are doing these things are Balinese with too much stress, over money or something, and it's made them a little mad."

"Ay!" said Darta. "This really is *bogbog*!"

"Think about it, Bli," said Suda. "How much do you have to make each month just to make ends meet?"

"The car. The telephone. The electricity. The water. The local tax. The TV. Interest to the bank. Bus fares for the children to get to school." Darta was adding it all up in his head. "About three hundred thousand rupiah." He turned to us. "That's a hundred and fifty dollars. And that's before I even buy a grain of rice. And the price of food here is soaring!"

"That's a lot of money," said Suda.

"I know. I have to find it all each month."

Jean and I were shocked. Suti, a school teacher with a good professional wage, made only a hundred dollars a month. "Thank god for Suti," I said.

"And Kadek," added Jean. The men nodded. "She must make a good salary at the water company."

"Still not enough," said Suda. "Ten years, even five years ago we needed almost nothing. Now there is so much inflation in Ubud that you have to be working with the tourists to survive. Nobody here farms anymore. No one can afford to. It all makes for a lot of stress." Being granted the opportunity to sit in on such a conversation was bitter-sweet. It was a privilege to be told of the family's struggles, but there was the nagging understanding that our presence was, in part, responsible for the problem. "There's a lot of money here in Ubud." Suda was talking directly to us now. "Many here are much richer than people I saw in America. That makes for a very special kind of stress. When you move from the village to the city, there is a clear change from farmer to office or factory worker. But it's not like that here. This is still a village. The community is still very strong, and community work takes up a lot of time. The stress comes from trying to run a business and fulfill your community obligations. It's hard when you can't answer the call of the *kulkul* bell. When you drive by in your car full of tourists while everyone is working to fix a road or prepare for a cremation, it doesn't feel good. It's embarrassing. Some people give money instead, but it's not the same as when you put the time in, and everyone knows it. I mean, look at the stress I'm under! The cost of building materials is going up so quickly that if I want to build some more bungalows in the rice fields, it's now or never." With that Suda got up and left.

"Who pissed on his cornflakes," I said as his silhouette disappeared down the path.

"Who what?" said Darta.

"Oh, nothing," I said.

"Are you going back soon?" he asked.

"No. We'll hang out here for a while," said Jean. "Right?" she asked me. I nodded.

"I'll go with Suda then," said Darta. He turned on his flashlight. "Do you have one?" he asked.

"Yes," we said, even though we didn't.

"Suda! Suda!" shouted Darta, jumping up. We watched as his flashlight beam jogged its way southward down the path.

"Afraid of the dark," said Jean. "He knew we'd still be here at midnight and couldn't stand the idea of going home alone."

"You think so?"

"I know so," she said. "Farmers have to be out here at night to control the water, but nobody else will risk meeting a ghost."

We flopped back onto the mat, Jean with her head on my shoulder. The moon was now directly overhead, and the first hint of a milky tide was preparing to wash the moon clean of its earth-shadow.

"Sometimes, like when Suda talks like that, I think it would have been better if I'd never come here," said Jean.

"It was the best thing you ever did," I said, "for you, for them, and for me."

"You didn't hear what Suda said?"

"I know you've seen this village change more than I have. Even I see how much it's grown. And it's very clear that this change in Ubud is the result of tourism. So it's easy for us to take the blame for what's going on here. But do we need to? Most of the changes in Bali are the result of the national economy. So do I need to take personal responsibility for Suda's hardships? Does that help?"

"Suda really touched a raw nerve in you," said Jean.

"This whole time in Indonesia has touched me. Last week you asked me to stand back from the emotional fire. I've tried to do that. I know we live on a small planet with a global economy, and I see that there's nowhere I can run to where my lifestyle choices won't affect Suda. So I might as well be here as anywhere else. You also said that if you've learnt anything from this family it's that you hang in there with those you love. All I can do for Suda is make a day-to-day commitment to be with him." I jumped to my feet. "C'mon. Let's roll up the mats and go home."

CHAPTER 10

Monkey Business

A week later we were sitting on the kitchen steps eating dinner when a nearby *kulkul* sounded. Tung. Ting. Tung-tung-tung-tung-tung-tung-tung... The double sounding of the bell followed by a rapid ringing meant there had been a robbery. Within moments the *kulkuls* of other nearby communities could be heard beating out the same message.

Darta flew out of his bedroom in just his underwear, ran to the pavilion to fetch his cleaver, and headed for the front gate. Almost as an afterthought, he ducked back into the room to fetch a sarong. Then he was off pounding down the steps and out into the night. There was a lot of shouting on the street and the starting of motorbikes. The main road north out of the village was already a roaring stream of traffic.

"Not again!" said Jean. "How much more of this can we all take?" She pushed her plate aside, leaving half her dinner, and stormed off back to our room. "I'm going to read," she said to the trees and the frogs.

I could ill afford such a display of emotion at the expense of my stomach. I finished my food and cleaned Jean's plate, too. By the time I was done, Ubud was quiet again. The streets were as silent as the grave. Ibu was weaving offerings on the Western Pavilion porch. I went over to ask her what was going on.

"I know as much as you do," she said. "We'll just have to wait and see."

"What are the offerings for?" I asked.

"Just something to do," she replied. "Keeping my fingers busy."

I imagined my mother or grandmother knitting her way through such a night. "I think Ubud's going crazy," I said.

"Maybe," said Ibu.

"Do you still think it's like it was in 1966?"

"Who told you I said that?" Her voice was round with surprise.

"I heard you say it. Jean heard you, too. A couple of weeks ago."

"I would never have said anything like that. This is all just very *biasa*."

Biasa literally means normal or usual. It is also shorthand for nothing to worry about or, perhaps, it's all just a storm in a tea cup. I was much relieved by Ibu's reassuring tone. The mother in any Balinese household is a pivotal personality. She quietly holds everything together and becomes the center about which everyone else rotates. Her authority is clear and well-respected. It needs no showy overstatement. I relayed Ibu's view of things back to Jean and she felt better, too.

Two hours later, just as we had fallen asleep, the *kulkuls* in every direction began sounding another alarm. Motorbikes and automobiles thundered northward again. Jean stuck her head under the pillow and went back to sleep. I lay awake listening to the alien sounds of late-night traffic. I waited to see how long it would be before everyone came back, but my eyelids grew heavy and I was soon asleep.

In the morning we were both up at first light, sitting on the kitchen steps like a pair of waifs, hungry both for breakfast and news of the previous night. Talking to Suti and the children as they all prepared for school gave us the barest outline of the story.

The lights of the Temple of the Dead in nearby Bentuyung had failed just after sunset. It being common knowledge that any self-respecting temple thief cuts power wires to conceal his activities, the lack of light caused all hell to break loose. Incensed that the thief had dared to strike so soon after sundown, every able-bodied man within five miles had been mobilized to comb the area. Witnesses had spoken of two cars containing five Javanese tourists that had stopped to view the temple that afternoon. Further questioning revealed that nobody had seen either of the cars leave the village, and yet neither were anywhere to be found! The search for the cars and their passengers had lasted three hours and turned up nothing. The crowd then dispersed, with small groups returning to their own villages to hang around on street corners or protect temples.

This much had been reported to the family when Darta had sneaked home from his post. But he had been off again at the second sounding of the *kulkul* and neither he nor Rudy had spoken to anyone since they returned home sometime in the early hours. Obviously, we would have to wait for a full account.

Our money was on Darta being the first up, but we still had to wait until nearly nine o'clock for him to open his bleary eyes and show his sleep-deprived face. He was in good spirits, but tired, and needed a wash and some coffee before he could spill any of his storyteller's beans. With his cup half-empty, he began to talk.

The *kulkul* had been rung a second time when someone saw a puff of smoke and the glow of a cigarette high up in a tall jackfruit tree next to Bentuyung's Temple of the Dead. The crowd regathered at the foot of the tree. "I saw him," said Darta. "The tree was perfectly still, not a branch or leaf moved. Even when nearby trees moved in the breeze, the jackfruit was still. Everyone was shining flashlights up into the top branches. These were strong flashlights, mostly brand new. But, this is funny." The tale had hardly started and already Darta was off chasing tangents. "The price of these big flashlights was fifteen thousand rupiah at lunch-time yesterday. People stopping to buy them on their way to Bentuyung the first time pushed the price up to seventeen thousand rupiah. When the *kulkul* rang the second time, only one or two smart shop owners were still open. From them, you couldn't get anything for less than twenty-five thousand!"

"So at least someone's doing well out of all of this," I said.

"In the tree, I saw a leg hanging down from a high branch, but nothing more, and that leg was quickly drawn up so I couldn't see it again. No one in the group had the courage to climb the tree. Out of five hundred men, nobody stepped forward. The thief might have had a knife, or worse, maybe a sickle. From above he could give a terrible wound. But no one was patient enough to outwait him either. He was in the high branches of a tree much taller than the others around it. He had nowhere to go but down. But the people wanted to get him right then and would not wait. So someone went to fetch axes.

"Then three trucks of police arrived. Even the Governor of the Gianyar district was there. He urged us not to kill the thief if we caught him. 'We need information more than we need revenge if we are to stop this group,' he said and asked for witnesses. Out of the five thousand people there, many went forward. Rudy went up since he was the only one in our family who had seen the leg.

"Then people started cutting down the tree. To one side of the tree was the temple. To the other was a small wood, and in front were open rice fields. They aimed to fell the tree into the rice fields, but it dropped toward the woods and got caught up in the other trees. The thief got away through the tree tops. Ah!

"The green shirt he had been wearing must have helped him. When I saw him earlier he had been in a green shirt, but it was hard to keep looking at it because it looked exactly like a big leaf. Many of us remembered that the old woman caught in the market-place robbery had worn an amulet. We were all talking about these people having magic protection."

Darta's monologue suddenly ran out of steam. Jean and I looked at each other, blank with amazement. It was hard to respond in any other way, especially considering all the contra-dictions in the testimony of a man trained as a lawyer. "You were all barking up the wrong tree!" was all I could think of to say.

Darta sensed our incredulity and quickly began back-ped-dling. "I said to everyone, 'If the thief saw us all standing here in the middle of the night, having just chopped down a perfectly good fruit-bearing tree, he'd really laugh. But it's OK. He's safe at home and never saw any of this.' But no one wanted to hear what I was saying."

Jean could no longer control herself and burst out laughing. I followed suit, and to his credit, so did Darta. "Oh, Darta," Jean gasped. "You're much better at *bogbog* than you ever would have been at law!"

"True," admitted Darta. "True enough. Suda said all along that it was just a monkey. He thought the red cigarette ember had been light from a flashlight reflected in one of the monkey's eyes, and that the smoke had been steam from the monkey pissing with fright, but none of us wanted to listen to him then. Do you think he might have been right?"

"Darta!" said Jean. "What kind of man would sit in a tree quietly smoking cigarettes with hundreds of armed men waiting below to cut him to pieces?"

Darta shrugged.

"Witness dismissed," I announced.

But the bard was not to be that easily put down. He started straight into another of his stories. "It reminds me of the time when the police came to the homestay across the street." He paused for effect and then continued. "Na. The younger brother of the owner was in his late twenties and always carried a long, sharp sword with him around the house. He was a little crazy and would sometimes swing the sword around fiercely. Some people were afraid he might run amok and kill someone, so the police were called. News of this spread around the neighborhood very, very quickly and everyone came out to see. Then six big policemen arrived from Gianyar in a truck. There were six hundred, maybe even a thousand people standing here in this little street waiting to see what would happen. The police went in and about five minutes later a man suddenly came running out into the street. No one remembers who he was. He just came running out into the crowd. Everyone thought he was the man running amok. So the crowd turned in front of him and went running down the street as well. Even people who had been sitting at home came out to join in. One old man down the street fell in his doorway and was trampled by his family, but that didn't matter—he was big and fat, like a mattress. As the crowd ran down to the crossroads, it got bigger and bigger. There it went past a meeting at the Tourist Information Office. Everyone there began running, too. That's where I joined in. I was coming home the other way. I didn't know what had happened, but felt that it was my duty to follow.

Fortunately, I was on the scooter and didn't have to run to keep up."

"How far did you all run?" I asked.

Darta waved his hand non-committally. All he would say was, "Down that way," leaving half of Ubud's population running through the streets of our imaginations. He was on a roll. "Once, we had a thief here, in this house."

"A third story?" I asked. "This really is our lucky day!"

"I can't just leave it at two," said Darta. "Two is unlucky. I have to tell a third. There was an Englishman who had a room here for six weeks. George was his name. When it came time for him to pay, he said he didn't have any money. He said money had been stolen from his room and he accused me and my family of taking it. He didn't want to pay for the room because he said I'd already taken the money. I was very angry with him and said that he was the thief because he wouldn't pay for the room. Next morning he took all his bags and jumped over the back wall into the woods. Someone saw him and asked what he was doing. He said, 'I'm leaving this homestay because they stole my money!'

"Also George was very sick during his stay with us. I had taken him to the doctor. But because he was so sick he hadn't changed any money and so owed the doctor forty thousand rupiah. When he hadn't paid in two weeks, the doctor came to me wanting me to go with him to the police to get George thrown out of Bali. By that time George had left. I didn't know where he was, but I told the doctor I could get the money if he would wait another week before going to the police. Then I sat and thought, 'Who could have taken his money?' I didn't believe anyone here had taken it, but couldn't think of anyone else. Then Ibu said she remembered seeing George's friend Gedé going into his room, and I became suspicious.

"So I went all over Ubud asking for Gedé, and eventually found him. I said, 'Gedé, I have a problem. George thinks I stole his money and he's going to the police. The doctor thinks George is a thief and he's going to the police. The police will then come and question me and there'll be many, many problems. They will ask me who else visited the home, and I will have to give them your name. I'm not worried for myself. I can answer all their questions and they'll know I'm honest. Policeman are well-trained. They know when they are hearing the truth and when they are being told a lie. So I'll be OK. But I want to warn you to get your story straight. I know you're an honest young man, but if you make a mistake when they question you, you will go to court. Everyone will see you, and then you will go to jail for maybe a year. If you have anything to say, I think it's better that you tell me now. Then only one person will ever know. Otherwise the police and everyone will know the truth.' Then Gedé said, 'Oh Darta! I took the money. Please help me. I'll give it back. I'll apologize.' I said, 'Here's what you must do. Write a letter saying what you did. Take it to George and confess.' He was so upset. I had to write the letter for him. Then I went home.

"Later, George and Gedé came to my house. As soon as they came in I started shouting at George. 'Get out! Get out of my home! You are a thief. You stole my money. I don't want you polluting my family home. Get out!' I went on and on like this. 'Oh Darta,' George said. 'I'm sorry. We found the money. You were right. You didn't steal it.' And he gave me the letter that I had written! I read it very slowly then turned to look at Gedé. 'Don't be angry with him,' said George. 'He took the money because his girlfriend needed an abortion.' I said, 'I know he's basically an honest man. I don't think he'll do it again.' I had told him to make up the story about the abortion.

"So George paid me the money he owed for the room and was very nice to me, but I still acted a little angry. I said he had to go and explain what had happened to everyone he had told, including the police. I wanted my family name cleared. And I wanted him to go and pay the doctor, too. He said he would go and do all of that right away and that he'd been suspicious of me because I had helped him so much! When he stayed here I often invited him to eat with us. Suti cooked for him when he was sick, and I took him to the doctor. He said he thought we were being kind to cover up the theft.

"Well, after that I thought about the only other theft we ever had here. An American called Andrew had two million rupiah in cash in his room and five hundred thousand had disappeared. Andrew said someone from the family must have taken it because a real thief would have taken it all. We all thought it was his Sumatran friend. Suda even confronted Andrew, and there was a big argument. Ibu said a real thief would only have taken a bit, just to make people think it was not a professional criminal.

"Na. Gedé was Andrew's friend, too. But I didn't go to him again straight away. I waited six months and then went to see him. 'Oh Darta!' he said. 'I took that money, too.' So again I made him write a letter. Then I looked up Andrew's address in the book we use to register our guests with the police, and sent him the letter. A few weeks later I got a reply saying that someone had just sent a letter and confessed. Andrew said that he was sorry for ever having suspected me.

Then I got a letter from George saying he was coming to Bali again for two weeks with his girlfriend and wanted to stay at my house to show no bad feelings. I said, 'Sure' and sent a car to meet him at the airport. I was polite to him when he arrived, but didn't offer him any food. He came with a very beautiful Thai woman. Rudy, Pung, and all the young men around here were always talking to her. George didn't like that. But where there's honey there'll be ants, and it seemed she was much more interested in Asian men. When George came to pay for his room after the first week, I charged him twenty thousand rupiah a day. 'It was only ten thousand rupiah last year,' he said. 'Yes,' I said. 'But it's twenty thousand now. Everywhere in Indonesia there is terrible inflation. Oh! Terrible inflation—twenty thousand.' He paid. What else could he do? Then he left and I've never heard from him again."

"Why did you help Gedé?" asked Jean.

"If someone in this family succumbed to temptation and took something," Darta said, "I wouldn't like to see them in jail. I'd hope someone would help them in the same way I helped Gedé."

It was late in the day and Jean and I were sitting on the little pavilion in the rice fields. "I wonder," I said. "Have they all been barking up the wrong tree, right from the beginning?"

"You mean, you think the thefts and beatings never happened?"

"Well, we know the robbery in the marketplace happened. We heard it, and know people who were there. But everything since then has been hearsay. Do you know anyone who actually saw what happened at Tegalalang or Pujung? The only situations people we know were actually involved in turned out to be hoaxes or mistakes. Did any of these events really happen?"

"I don't know," Jean said. "I never thought to question any of it."

"Neither did I. It was Suda's theory about last night's monkey business that got me thinking. Then there was Darta's story about the stampede; that was all over nothing, too. I'm not saying that nothing happened. We saw them all out on the streets every night, but maybe we didn't see it accurately."

"What did we see then?"

"I don't know. That's what I'm asking." We fell silent for a while, watching the sunset. "The way Darta dealt with Gedé says a lot about this culture: George was the perceived threat to the harmony, not Gedé."

"Hmm," said Jean. "And think of what Suda said on the night of the eclipse. Think of this small group of Hindus beside Java's huge Islamic population. Suda told us how hard it's been to hold this community together. Maybe they needed this drama, for themselves. 'We're banded together. We're ferocious!' It's like a football team psyching itself up—'Let's go give 'em hell!'—They kept the Dutch out for hundreds of years like this. I don't think they're conscious of it now, but they've given themselves and the world a strong message about how fiercely they'll protect their culture. It's like psychic armor."

"You know," I said, "you may be right."

"We almost didn't trust them, did we?"

"It is all a matter of trust, isn't it?"

"I feel that's what I'm learning from this," said Jean.

"We could rush back to America or England and pour ourselves into a new life there, which I'm not yet ready to do, or we could just go with the flow, stay here a bit longer, and trust what's happening to us. It's like being a Balinese child. Do you remember the story you tell about the babies here?" Jean shook her head.

"You often tell new visitors how a baby is passed from mother to father to sibling to grandparent, to anyone who comes by, but is never put down."

"I tell that story a lot?" said Jean.

"Then you invite whoever's listening to imagine what it would feel like to be a child who was always cuddled and never left alone. You ask them how they would feel and they usually say how secure and full of trust they would be. Then you talk about the way this is enshrined in Balinese culture: how a child is rarely put down during the first three months of its life, until the 'Touching the Ground' ceremony. You say the children are always loved and cared for because the Balinese believe that a baby has just come from God. You talk about how close everyone is and how a Balinese family all sleeps in one bed—like little snakes, you always say. You talk about how people support each other and how they come to trust life."

"I say all that?"

"Yes, you do."

"But I don't think they understand trust in the same way we do," said Jean. "By our standards they often appear to be terrible at keeping their word! We say, 'I trusted them and they broke their word,' end of story. But their stories are epics, they go on and on. They have to keep living together, at the community hall, in the family compound, on the street. In our culture we can break with family or neighbors. No big deal. But for any big ceremony here, a family needs the help of almost everyone else in the village, and sometimes family as far as second cousins. I don't even know who my second cousins are."

"I don't even know most of my first cousins! I think that's part of it, it's a question of scale. Perhaps the Balinese see trust on a different scale. They trust that somehow it will all come together in the end, in spite of personalities and setbacks. They trust people to be whoever they are—Gedé is a thief. They don't throw him in jail, they just don't leave anything lying around for him to take— and they trust life to be good to them. I think this sense of trust must come from their deep sense of community. It flowers all on its own. The work is in making the community, and the Balinese work very, very hard at that. The community exists beyond everyone's personal dramas, but still responds to them. The temple ceremonies happen reliably, come what may, every two hundred and ten days, and everyone goes. And everyone pulls together for cremations. Right from birth, their sense of trust is based on something bigger than their own lives."

We were quiet then, Jean and I, and the rice fields and the white herons, and the sunset.

For the family, all the furor surrounding the Bentuyung temple incident had been eclipsed by the worsening health of Suti's grandfather. Nobody, himself included, knew exactly how old he was. But he was the only person Darta knew who remembered the Dutch invasion of southern Bali in 1906. He certainly remembered Ubud in the 1930s and often told stories about the handful of Western painters and musicians who helped establish the village as a center of culture and tourism.

"Grandfather's wanted to die for years," said Darta, "ever since he broke his leg at a wedding. It never healed well and he's been unable to walk. He's the last of his generation still alive; he cried when each one of his friends left without him. A month ago he had a heavy stroke and has been ready to go ever since." This much was not news to us. We knew of the stroke, how the old man had been rushed to hospital in Denpasar, and that he had been on a drip-feed ever since. "After coming home he began refusing food," Darta continued. "Then I was visiting him late one evening last week. We were alone and I saw him reach over with his good arm and pull the tube out. Who was I to stop him? He pulled the tube out and then looked at me. I smiled, turned the light out, shut his door behind me, and went home.

"Next morning Suti's brother, who would do anything to keep the old man alive, came to me in a panic. 'He pulled the tube out! He pulled the tube out!' he kept saying. They had just discovered it. I pretended shock and confusion, but made sure they didn't put the drip back in. He was ready to go. Who were we to stop him?

"The neighbors wanted him to hang on long enough for them to begin their family temple ceremony. They never said anything, of course, but we all knew they had spent a lot of money repairing their shrines and preparing for a big celebration. If grandfather died before they began, they wouldn't be able to start at all. Neighbors have to mourn for seven days after a death and can't make or attend any ceremonies during that time. All their work would have been for nothing. They were so pleased when the Brahmana high priest came today to start their ceremony. Now that they have begun, the old man is free to die."

Suti's grandfather died that night. The family spent the next morning laying out the body. Unlike Pung's mother, who had been cremated immediately, the old man was to "rest in the ground" while money was gathered for a full cremation. As the corpse was washed and anointed in preparation for its burial, Adé was right there, prodding the body and poking at the bent nose. When they used string to tie the old man's mouth shut, Adé said to Darta, "You're going to die, too, aren't you, Pan Abut? And you won't have any teeth either. And when you're dead we're going to have to tie your mouth shut with string, too."

With Suda responsible for coordinating community involvement in any death rites, Adé had frequent opportunities to attend such events. A month rarely went by without his father being called upon to perform his duties.

We told Suti how sorry we had been to hear of her grandfather's death. Suti was quite surprised by our concern. "Don't be sorry," she said. "It was expected. He was very old." It wasn't that she was untouched by grief, rather that deep grief was more appropriate for untimely deaths.

When community and extended family life makes you intimate with several thousand people, joy and tragedy can follow sharply upon one another's heels. Our time in Bali had been a precipitous roller-coaster journey between these highs and lows. The challenge was to partake in the drama in such a way that we could find within ourselves the trust in life that a Balinese child finds in its family's arms, and never loses.

Jean and I began talking more and more seriously about finding a way to make Ubud our home. We even booked and paid for a return trip to Singapore, extending our stay in Bali by at least another two months.

It helped that community focus was moving away from the issue of the temple thievery. Enthusiasm for spending full nights wandering the streets had waned to the point that a schedule had been drawn up. Each family head was detailed with responsibility to participate in the guarding of a temple for one night a week, and a fine of five thousand rupiah for lack of attendance had been instituted. In practice this meant that many unmarried younger brothers were sent as substitutes. Nevertheless, through nights together with nothing better to do than talk, the men of Ubud began rediscovering the sense of community that the pressures of tourism had been steadily eroding. An expensive series of temple renovations were proposed, ostensibly to secure temple valuables, but also as an expression of a renewed sense of pride in their village. The basic plan was to rebuild the shrines where the sacred objects of each temple were kept. The facades would maintain their traditional elegance and beauty, but huge cement-clad safes and many thousands of dollars worth of electronic alarm equipment would also be installed. And while they were at it, the village decided to renovate everything else about each of the temples as well. With each part of the village responsible for a different temple, the former aggression changed into friendly, though intense, rivalry regarding the building work.

This new energy came to express itself in the form of organized work days, during which the village men did the basic laboring prior to the higher-quality craftsman's work. Eventually this spirit also gave birth to a new public performance in the outer courtyard of the Temple of the Dead. The men of North Ubud banded together, practiced for a couple of months, and began performing the *kecak*—a one-hundred-and-twenty-man chorus accompanied by the dancing of the Ramayana. They did it for fun, and for the sense of togetherness it engendered. All proceeds went to the temple.

Though no one was ready to admit it so quickly after the events in Bentuyung, Darta would soon come to describe this time as "a storm on a molehill."

CHAPTER 11

A House in Bali

Ubud began to calm down, and we regained our interest in wandering abroad, seeing the countryside, and visiting friends. The loop through the fields to Suda's house took us north along the path where the eclipse party was held and across a small viaduct. Looking down, I always marveled at the six-foot wide, sixty-foot deep fissure the stream had carved for itself. I understood the Balinese superstitions about such places. It made sense that they were the realm of ghosts and spirits, goblins and fairies. Beyond the viaduct we turned south, walking back toward Ubud. After crossing the main road, we went down the single-track dirt road to the family rice fields where Suda lived.

When I first came to Bali, only Ibu's brother, Paman, had lived here. He had a small shack surrounded by banana trees and tapioca plants at the back of the field. Everyone else stayed at the family house. But as the children grew, this arrangement became more and more intolerable. There just wasn't enough room. Suda, Kadek, Turia, Adé, and Pung then moved to the rice field, building two makeshift bamboo and thatch huts next to Paman's. Within a year the family had saved enough money to build something more permanent. Suda built two dingy rooms to rent to tourists. They generated little income and were occupied only in July and August when everything else in Ubud was full. After another year, he used more of the family savings to build himself a small three-room house and a kitchen up by the dirt road. Suda and his family lived here while Pung and Paman continued to stay in the huts at the back, next to the empty tourist rooms.

A further investment built a poolroom from which Suda and Pung earned a few rupiah to buy rice. When the Cheap & Cheerful Café had been at the height of its success, a pool table had been added at the back. As one of the first tables in Ubud, and being in the center of a busy neighborhood, it did remarkable business, clearing up to fifty thousand rupiah a night. When Kadek's mother retired from her office job, she decided she wanted to run both the café and the poolroom, which were actually in her family compound. It was soon after this that Suda moved to the rice field. He and Pung then decided to buy another table. Both borrowed heavily, but failed to see a return. Their new situation was too remote. The table was well-used, but by a small group of local teenagers with more time on their hands than money in their pockets.

Suda was very philosophical about it all. "My house is very simple. There's no place for friends or guests to stay. Many of my friends have big homes and a nice place to sit and drink coffee. They are all much more successful than me, but all they talk about is money, building another room and buying another car. It's a boring conversation. It would be better if they had another story."

"Well, at least you have the moon-viewing pavilion. I'm sure none of them have one," said Jean.

Suda smiled. "Ya. It's enough." He had erected the small, square moon-viewing pavilion back near the huts. It was made and thatched with second-hand materials salvaged after repairs had been made at one of the village temples. From time to time he would take one of the seats out of the family minibus and put it in the pavilion so he could sit with Kadek to watch the moon rise. "My friends are always running around, but I just stay in the rice field. If people want to talk to me, they know where to find me. I'm just in the rice field."

We visited him often. If the late afternoon sky had no moon, we would turn to watch the sunset. Conversation wandered far and wide. One evening we talked about a new addition to the household, a young man living in the huts at the back with Pung and Paman.

154

"Nengah?" said Suda. "He's from Karangasem. He used to work at a restaurant in Candi Dasa. Something happened there and he came to Ubud looking for work. He came to me because he thought I still had the café. Well, I couldn't give him any work, but I could give him a place to stay. 'When you want to eat, please come and eat with us,' I said. If I have a little money, of course I'll share it with him. But when we have nothing, there'll be nothing for him either.

"My thinking is not very Western. I'm very backward that way. But I do as my father used to. After Mount Agung erupted in 1963, our house was full of the refugees Roda took in. After that, those people were always coming to look for Roda, bringing him chickens and rice and things. There were other examples, too. When I was in Java, the people I stayed with took no rent for a whole year. I was so embarrassed I had to leave. And when I left, they cried. I will always remember how generous they were to me. Pedicab drivers, stall holders, everyone was so helpful.

"Roda's principle was this: Give to others, and don't worry if you never get anything in return. He just did it knowing that if he helped someone else's children, then his children would also be taken care of. I often think about this. I ask myself, how come I was so lucky in Java? How is it that I met you and that I was able to see America? This is Roda's karma. So I give Nengah a bed to sleep in, because now he needs it. It's about karma, because I hope people will be good to Turia and Adé, too."

I had always liked Suda, but considered him something of a brooder. In the comfort of his own home, however, he was relaxed, open and animated. I realized how heavily the pressures of the family home had weighed upon him.

"After University I went to work in Borneo. I was one of four boys in the family, and I thought it would be hard for us all to make a living in Ubud. So I went to find work with the idea that when I had enough money, I could call other family members to come and join me. In 1980, I took a job in the administration of the harbor at Balikpapan. I worked there for a year before moving to Central Java. Then Paman came to tell me Roda was ill. I came back with him and didn't leave Ubud again. Darta said it was time for me to stop chasing dreams. He persuaded me to stay and marry Kadek.

"Between Borneo and America, I've seen the bottom and top of how life can be. But I don't usually talk about these things. I don't say to people that I went to America. I say that I learned my English from the TV. I don't want to appear arrogant. But now I wonder why I had all those experiences. What were they for? I know I don't want to be at the bottom, and I'm happier here than I could possibly be in America, but whenever I get to the top of a hill I see another hilltop ahead, and always I want to chase that next peak. I have this appetite, but I want to live simply, too. I liked living in the huts and didn't care about the chicken mites or the mice. I would have stayed there, but Kadek wanted more.

"When I meet other Balinese who have been to America, I let them talk about L.A., San Francisco or New York. I ask questions as if I've never heard of the places before, even though I've probably seen much more of America than they have. They need to be the experts more than I do, and I want them to be happy more than I need to talk about what I've seen."

If Suda wasn't at home when we went to visit, we sat on his kitchen step, overlooking the rice field. "Jean," I said one afternoon, "do you feel embarrassed when Suda talks about how little he has, considering how much we have in comparison?"

"He could make money, he could have a job if he wanted to, but he prefers to work for the community."

"He doesn't really need to work with Kadek bringing home a salary, does he?"

"It's tight. Remember what he said during the eclipse? But he chooses this and she understands. And I've never felt that either of them begrudge us what we have. If nothing else, when Suda was in America he learned how hard people have to work to make a living. He knows it's not all money and holidays for Westerners."

"He's much more relaxed than when he was living at the family home, isn't he?" I said. "That knot has gone from between his brows. It was too small a space for him and Darta. Two big personalities, not enough space. But that 'appetite' still gnaws at him. He still seems a little lost, doesn't he?"

"He doesn't really like working with the tourists, and he can't be a farmer anymore. With three crops a year squeezed out of this land, ten percent going to the harvesters and then milling fees, he says the profit is only about one hundred and twenty thousand rupiah a harvest. The rice price is fixed by the government and was a good price ten years ago, but it isn't anymore, not here in Ubud. The rice from this land isn't even enough to feed his family."

"There must be a lot of pressure for him to build here."

"That's another thing he said during the eclipse," said Jean. "But he wants to stay as simple as he can. They'll keep this land in rice as long as Paman is alive. Paman farms it and loves it."

We will never know whether it was the late afternoon conversations that provoked Suda to action, but what he chose to do, and our response to what he did, bound our fates even more closely together. He didn't mention what he was planning, and perhaps didn't even know himself until he started. Even then, the only signs of his internal machinations were the sudden appearance of a large pile of bricks and an even larger mound of sand by his front door.

"Do we just have to watch him do this?" I said as we stood before the sand.

"Absolutely not. We have to save him from himself. If he follows his own design he'll lose a lot of money. We must at least help him make something that someone will want to stay in!"

We found Kadek in the kitchen and she confirmed our deepest fears. Suda planned to build some small, cheap rooms where the huts stood. "Very basic," she said, "to rent out very cheap. He thinks if he can make rooms like the two already there, and rent them cheaper, people will come."

"It used to be mostly backpackers coming to Ubud," said Jean. "People stayed for months at a time and were looking for the cheapest possible room. But that's changing. People fly to Bali, come to Ubud, and stay for two weeks. They've got more money than people who are on the road for a year. Ubud is going up-market, not down. Almost every family compound has a sign saying 'Room for Rent.' Suda could do something different. He could build a house—a proper house. Get a long-term renter; make a real income."

We sat on the kitchen step, ignoring a spectacular sunset while imagining various styles of construction at the other end of the field. "He wants to build where the huts are," said Jean. "That's a good idea, so no more rice field is taken out of production. The huts are bamboo, so they can be carried up here."

Ever pragmatic, I was wondering how Suda could make money: "The less he spends, the quicker the return. A single-story building or buildings, simple construction, elegant design."

"No. It needs a second floor," mused Jean. "I want to be able to lay in bed to watch the sunrise and the sunset."

" 'I' want to lay in bed and watch the sunrise?"

"I said 'I'?"

I nodded.

She thought for a moment, shrugged, and said, "Well, why not?"

"Suda! Suda!" Jean called him over as soon as he got home. "I've got an idea I want to share with you." Her speech lasted ten minutes and was very persuasive. Suda held up his hands in mock defeat the moment she stopped talking.

"You're right. I'd make a big mess of it." The Balinese lack of attachment to things always amazed me. "Do it. Do whatever you want with it. It's all yours."

"My God," I said. "We're going to have a house in Bali."

A few days later we spoke more formally to Suda and Darta at the family house. "Darta," began Jean. "If we build this house, I want to make an agreement that will be fair. I don't want to lease the land, but I don't want there to be room for you to think, even in the farthest corner of your mind, about how much money you could have made if you had leased the land to someone else."

I felt a little left out that Jean was talking about an "I" instead of a "we," but I also recognized that it was the depth of her personal connection with Darta that would make this all possible.

"You are right, Jean," said Darta. "Right from the start we must think about all the details so that time doesn't make them into big problems. I will not lease this land, to you or to anybody else. It must be for my family, and what is built on it must be for my family, too."

"Yes. I see this as a joint venture."

"Joint venture? I'm sorry Jean, but I have to tell you I haven't yet seen a joint venture that works. 'I have the land; you have the money.' The Balinese always lose their ability to earn a living from their land. I see the journey more like this." Darta held up his two index fingers, side by side. "I want for us to continue to be close. Very, very close. But always there must be a space between us. Even if small, a space must continue to exist. If we allow our paths to cross, if we come to believe that there is perfect agreement, then we will be mistaken. Look." He crossed his index fingers. "When the paths cross, they can rub together." He hunched his shoulders, rubbed his fingers together, and looked right into the place where his fingers met. "Where they rub together, there will be heat, and soon a fire. Our interests must remain closely related, but separate. This is not about how to share this home and this land, which must remain with my family. But you must get your money's worth so that you are satisfied with your investment. We need to agree on these things."

"We'll say that our money buys us so many months a year over five years," I said.

"Yes. It must be like that. We are close, but there will be problems, small and big problems. We must expect to deal with them if we are all to be satisfied in the end. Five years is good. If we say twenty years and I die, who knows if you will be close to my son. In five years we will talk again. This way Suda and I are the building contractors. We are building our own house so there is no reason to charge you for twenty-five trucks of sand when twenty are used, or twenty-two hours of labor when twenty are worked. That's why Westerners' houses always cost more than planned; the owner is making money from his land while he still can."

"And you won't gain anything by inflating the price," I said, "when you have to give me the value of my investment in months of rental."

"Parallel, but no fire point." He and Suda had obviously talked long and hard about this. "I wouldn't think of doing this with anyone else," Darta said. We were flattered.

We were also very excited. We rushed back to our room and Jean pulled out a few sketches she had made on some rough paper. We pored over them between cups of tea.

"He doesn't want to lease us the land," summarized Jean, "but he does want an ongoing income. And we're looking for an arrangement that will be good for us, too." She reached for a pen and some more paper and began to write:

Rental Agreement
This is an agreement between the parties of Wayan Sudarta, Nyoman Suda Riasta and family, and Jean and William Ingram on this day, May 25th, 1993, in Ubud, Bali, Indonesia.

Term
This contract begins January 1st, 1994, and concludes when the sum total of the Ingrams' investment (as stipulated in this agreement) has been repaid or at the end of 5 years. The contract can thereafter be renegotiated between both parties...

"You write legalese!"
"I used to run a business. I wrote contracts all the time."
By bedtime there were three-page drafts plus a page of questions in both English and Indonesian. We felt we'd covered all the bases: our investment was to be regarded as a loan to be repaid

over five years. The number of months we were entitled to was to be determined by dividing the value of this loan by an agreed rent. To make everything easy, we would agree that interest on the loan and inflation in the rent would cancel each other out. If we were unable to come to Bali, we could sublet. We could also sublet even if we were still in Bali. If the income from this was more than the rent we had agreed with Darta and Suda, the difference would be split between us and the family. If there was a breakdown in our relationship with the family, they could buy back the remainder of the lease, plus interest of X percent per annum; the percentage was to be negotiated before signing the contract. There was to be no building in the rice field in front of the house; if this happened, the family had to buy back the rest of the lease. During the periods we were not in Bali, the family could rent the house out for as much money as they could get, but we had first choice, each year, of the months we wanted—no long-term renter could usurp our right.

Over coffee the next morning, we called the brothers together on our porch and presented them with the fruits of our evening's labor.

"Only a first draft," said Jean. "Just something to start us thinking along the right lines."

As they began to read, Darta's forehead creased into a deep frown. He took his coffee and moved to the kitchen. Suda turned white, got up, and left the compound entirely.

"Oops!" I said.

It was two hours before they were ready to speak again.

"I can't sign anything like this," said Suda. "All these horrible events you imagine happening; I would feel like an evil man putting my name to this—like I might turn into someone who would do these things to you." I started feeling very small and humble. "We've all known each other for, what, eight years. There is a level of trust and understanding."

"When we said agreement," injected Darta, "we meant that we agree, here at the outset, that whatever problems may arise between us over this house, we will sit down together and talk it through until a solution is found. We want an agreement to agree. You are family, and this is how a family should work. I am not a perfect man. Don't ever trust me a hundred percent. It is certain that there will be problems. But we will work them out. Please trust me this much." Jean and I almost cried. "The land over there has no certificate, you know," he continued. "It's been registered with the government, but when Roda said we should go and get a certificate, I said no. I've seen what can happen. There were two brothers and they were really close. Wayan was a hard worker and bought land with his money. Madé wasn't a hard worker and liked to sit and talk. When Wayan bought the land, he put it in Madé's name because he loved him. 'I want this to be your land,' he said. When the brothers got old and died and it was time for the children to inherit, Madé's son took everything and threw his cousin off the land.

"I don't want pieces of paper to become weapons within this family or between us and you. A certificate is only needed to sell the land, or to borrow money from a bank with the land as a guarantee. If there is a good relationship, paper will get in the way more than it will help. If you live only on paper, you forget how to be together in real life."

Jean and I were given much pause for thought. Were we willing to risk ten or fifteen thousand dollars on a handshake? It was clear that we stood to gain more than a home in Bali. There was also an opportunity to regain a degree of faith and trust in people that, as Suda noted in America, has been long since lost in the West.

"I would have a lawyer draw up contracts even if I were doing something with my brother!" I said to Jean.

"Yes. And I think there's much more to win here than there is to lose. I love what Darta said about not trusting him a hundred percent. It makes me think of that watch he wears, the one he tells everyone Roda bought in 1946, after the Japanese left. You know this story? He says his father decided to buy a watch, and saved up three months salary to do so. During that time, Darta claims there was no food in the house and the children had to go into the fields to catch insects and pick leaves. The truth is, a tourist gave that watch to Darta in 1980. He wasn't even born in 1946!"

"Hang on. You say 'love' and 'trust' and then show Darta to be a liar?"

"Their words may change with the wind, they certainly know that about themselves. But they trust their own hearts, and they trust our hearts. And they're asking us to do the same.

"So, it's kind of like getting married again."

"Are you ready for this, then?"

"I think we left Tokyo looking for something like this—this kind of community. I'm not going to turn and run now."

In a subsequent conversation, Darta offered us the use of the house whenever we were in Bali. "Even if we stay ten months each year?" I asked.

"Especially if you stay a long time," he said. "The worst case for me is that I lose the use of my land because you are on it. And I am ready for that. For you it would be that you lose the use of your money because you don't come to Bali. If we can all be clear about that now, things will be easier, whatever happens. Do you agree? Your money, my land, both lost? Then whatever we get will be a bonus." We agreed. "I've told the other brothers that the piece of land at the back is my share. If it ever comes to carving the land up between us, you're with me. So think of this as your land and your home. Stay here as long as you want."

Our intention was also that the house should provide income for the family if we were ever to stop coming to Bali. In truth, our presence in the family compound had always brought in a considerable income. The family had a superstition that with Jean present the rental rooms were always full, and for years it had been next to impossible for her to get Darta to accept any rent. Numerous little business ventures and local tour ideas bringing together Jean's entrepreneurial flair and Darta's local knowledge had also paid rich dividends for the family. So friendship aside, it was a sound investment and in everyone's interest for us all to live in each other's pockets.

The family home had always been a stimulating place to be, but it was hard to focus on designing a house while staying there. The distractions were constant. The idea of building a house in Bali had given birth to many sibling thoughts regarding the challenges of making a living. And the more we thought about all of that, the more we felt in need of the more private space a house could offer. Circular logic it may have been, but it turned a dream into a firm commitment. We had pulled ourselves up by our own bootstraps and were suddenly ready to set up on our own.

"Kind of sad, isn't it," I said to Jean. "We've done and learned so much here, in the family home. It's the end of an era."

"Yes. And the beginning of one, too."

We went to the beach for a week to draw up plans. Nothing fancy, just a rough outline showing where to put the walls, windows and doors. Further detail concerning plumbing and wiring could wait until later. We bought the biggest pad of paper we could find, a few pencils, a ruler, and a lot of erasers. Jean's design parameters required the inclusion of a large open dining room that could double as a yoga space, and an upstairs bedroom from where we could watch sunrise and sunset. I wanted a well-lit office for my writing, door frames high enough not to concuss me, and kitchen and bathroom counters tall enough for me to use without putting my lower back into spasm.

Building in the garden at the back of the rice field, with the house overlooking the family land, would clearly link the value of the property to the view. We hoped that constructing one house would save the rest of the land from development. The idea of duplicating the Ungaran organic farm had changed somewhat over the course of two months, but our wish to see the land remain under plough stayed as strong as ever.

It was a challenge to design a structure that fulfilled all these requirements and fit in the garden. Three days of heated seaside discussion and cooling dips in the ocean were needed before we had something we wanted to go back with and map out on the ground in Ubud.

Plotting these ideas out around the still-standing huts with string and a two-meter tape measure was an extra challenge. When Suda first introduced us to a contractor, our plan was still more intuitive than actual. He seemed perfectly unruffled by our lack of clarity and agreed on a price even without a final drawing.

His attitude felt consistent with our original gut feeling to build the house and our faith that we would somehow find an income to enable us to live in it. We would finance the building from savings made while working in Japan.

"I want to start work right now," the contractor said, "and you don't have all your drawings finished yet. So draw the ground plan today, because I'll need to know about it first to dig foundations. Then draw me the windows and doors so I can start on the walls. While we're doing all that, get the roof drawings ready. Just keep one step ahead of me and we'll be OK." Far from being upset, he seemed relieved by our approach. Balinese often seem to prefer slap-dash over careful planning, but his enthusiasm for bush-whacking made me nervous. I got butterflies all the way down into my wallet.

All of this urgency, however, was tempered by the need to wait for an auspicious day to lay the foundations. The local priest was consulted. The next good day was still a week away, just prior to our visa run to Singapore. This gave Paman and Pung time to gather some friends and carry their huts up to the front by Suda's house. It also gave enough time for a Javanese work crew to dig the foundation trenches and for Jean and me to get our drawings together. My high-school technical drawing classes served me well as I plotted out plans, elevations, and isometric projections of the structure. My drawings were pin-point accurate, and the contractor found them totally unreadable. Jean's unique perspective on reality produced aerial views of each room with every wall pealed open and laid flat like the petals of a pressed flower. Every internal detail revealed itself as you slowly rotated the paper. The builders always laughed at Jean's designs but understood them immediately, and always chose to use her drawings over mine.

Auspicious days are always busy days for a priest, and long boring days for anyone dressed up in a sarong waiting for him. We were ready for the priest at about two. He arrived a little after six. The offering of coffee and cigarettes was perfunctory since he still had three more calls to make. The ceremony was quickly under way.

The priest, dressed in white with a yellow hip cloth, squatted in the northeast corner of the foundation trench. Beside him were baskets of Ibu's offerings and burning incense. Above him stood a makeshift bamboo shrine which Paman had built. The central offerings were a pair of bricks to go under the foundation, a whole coconut, an unbroken egg, and some old Chinese coins. Following the prayers, mantras, and the sprinkling of holy water and palm wine, the priest inscribed an Om symbol in a lotus flower on one of the bricks. A number of smaller woven palm-leaf offerings were then neatly sandwiched between the bricks and laid in the trench. On top of this was placed a bucket-shaped palm-leaf offering that contained the coconut, the egg and the coins. "To Ibu Pertiwi, the Earth Mother," said Ibu, "asking her for permission to build here." Meanwhile Paman had taken the remaining offerings and placed them in the shrine. With a few muttered words and the pouring of various holy fluids upon this altar, the blessings of the local deities were appropriated. The ceremony was then brought to a close, and we were deemed free to lay brick and pour cement at will. Bureaucracy in Bali being what it was, this was the only "official" level of permission needed for us to start a small-scale building project.

No further work was begun before our trip to Singapore. Nyoman, the contractor, merely came over to Suda's for the signing of the contract and initialing of a photocopy pastiche of my drawings and Jean's color-coordinated mind maps. These were to serve as the final plans. As Pung drove us down to the airport, we were bubbling with a mixture of anticipation and trepidation.

Our flight to Singapore took us via Jakarta, which had us reminiscing about all that had happened in the two extremely full months since we had last been there. Our continuing journey from Jakarta started out across the vast water-lacy edges of southern Sumatra. The skies we traversed were clear, and from twenty-five thousand feet we looked down on a broad, sun-bleached land.

"Why are the rivers so brown?" Jean asked me. "They're huge. Look." I peered over her shoulder and out the window. "This one, and that one there. They're as wide as my thigh!" We looked more closely as the world slipped by beneath us. Heavily silted rivers meandered across a flat, uninteresting landscape. What there was to see was clearly man-made: a bursting township swelling around a crook in one of the rivers; narrow checker-board strips of drab green and olive-gray cultivation clinging to needle-thin runnels of irrigation water. "All of this was once forest," Jean said.

The sense of devastation was redoubled when we crossed a laser-straight line, running from beneath the plane to beyond the horizon. It sliced a division between the drab expressions of progress and a virgin jungle. The forest's rivers were a gleaming lapis blue in a quilt of emerald green. Whereas the logged-out landscape shimmered beneath a heat haze, the forest stood comfortably in the shade of its own fluffy white expirations.

When a flight attendant handed us the first newspaper we had seen for weeks, we found it to be full of depressing news. We read of immense forest fires in both Sumatra and Indonesian Borneo. The smoke was so bad it had grounded all air traffic in and out of Borneo and was causing smog alerts five hundred miles away, across the sea in Singapore.

Being in Singapore did little to relieve our despondency. Old neighborhoods were being leveled left and right for the erection of high-rise housing and high-priced malls. Culture shock was painfully intense. In the lines of every skyscraper we saw the edge of the clear-cut. In the hiss of each subway train we heard the echoes of chain-saws. We could not wait to leave.

Fortunately, our flight back to Bali avoided Sumatra, and we had time to talk. The over-development and deforestation we had seen were not other people's problems; the plan to build a house made it all very personal. We had left Suda money for materials that would be on-site by the time we returned. We realized we were committed to the process, even if only to ensure that good use would be made of the natural resources involved. We restated our decision to avoid rain forest lumber, diverted money from the building to the garden budget, decided on simple cement floors instead of expensive tile, and promised Mother Earth not to overindulge in needless decorative flourishes. Small, simple, and elegant became the design criteria.

By the time we got home, Nyoman's crew had left for the night. We stood in the gathering dusk surveying their work. They had already re-dug the foundations and poured a considerable amount of cement.

"What are they doing?" I asked no one in particular. "The foundations were perfect before we left. Why did they change it?"

Jean counseled me against beginning our relationship with the building crew with an explosion of temper and suggested I wait to hear their side of the story. It turned out that they had no story and were just following Nyoman's directions. We politely confronted Nyoman, who responded by asking us to show him, on the ground, what we had really wanted. With the notched length of bamboo that they were using as a measure, we marked out the foundations once again.

"Well, that's exactly how they were before we started!" said Nyoman full of surprise.

"Oh, brother," I said under my breath.

"It's OK. We'll just dig this all up and start again," Nyoman continued. "We'll be back on track by tomorrow morning."

Keeping the foundations on track took a lot more supervision than we had expected, especially considering that we had employed a contractor to do that for us. As the walls began to rise we were constantly finding blank surfaces where door and window frames should have been. They even started constructing one room without any doors or windows at all.

The riot act was read to poor Nyoman at least once a day for more than two weeks, and on each occasion he apologized and agreed to do the corrective work at his own expense. Then one morning I came in and looked over his shoulder at the plans he was working from. They were the preliminary sketches we had given him the first time we met. I pulled my copy of the final plans out of my pocket. "Where is your set of these?" I asked.

Nyoman looked very forlorn. He ran his hand almost lovingly across my set of drawings and said, "Oh. I've seen you with these. And I've wanted so much to have a set for myself. It would make this job so much easier."

I spun around and bellowed across the rice field, "Suda! Suda. Where the hell are Nyoman's drawings!"

I heard Suda whoop. "OK. OK," he shouted. There was both embarrassment and laughter in his voice. I saw him go into his room and a few minutes later he came running down the path. He came to a halt before us, smiling broadly, and handed Nyoman his plans.

"Where were they?" I asked.

"Under my mattress."

"Why?"

Suda shrugged. "Safe-keeping?"

Once Nyoman had his copy in hand, things went more smoothly. We still found small mistakes, like the odd window frame set inside out, but these suddenly seemed like minor issues. What remained a mystery was the alarming rate at which the house was expanding beyond its original parameters. With the purchase of a builder's tape measure, we discovered that one side of the kitchen was a foot longer than the other, and that the front porch had grown by almost three times that margin in each direction. A little trigonometry further proved that the house did not contain a single right angle. Since no one had ever claimed it would, this quickly became a non-issue. After some basic interrogation of the work force, we reassured ourselves that the reason all this was happening was due to nothing more malicious than poor work-manship. It took a little longer to figure out why everything was being built almost twenty percent over size. We had stressed over and over that we wanted doors that would be large enough not to shave the top off my head. That everything was getting so big was, we thought, due to an over-enthusiastic application of this rule of thumb. Suda told us Nyoman was following tradition by using my size as the basic unit by which all other measurements in the structure would be standardized. Whatever the reason, we were getting a very big house. Everyone who came to view it, Balinese or Western, congratulated us on its stature, said they had not known we were planning to open a restaurant, and asked where our new house was.

Watching all the materials required for this extravagance as they were hand-carried across the rice field to the building site was at times excruciating. I wondered about all the naturally beautiful places that were probably being destroyed to make this spot beautiful for us. Our bird's-eye vantage point over Sumatra had faced us with the reality of our relationship with the environment. Intellectually, we both knew that there was nothing else to do but continue. "Our best is the best we can do," we reminded ourselves. But this didn't really help.

We started to take our study of Balinese more seriously, studying two or three times a week with Wayan, a teacher in South Ubud. Being away from the building site and back into the culture was a welcome relief.

The course started with an exposition of the linguistic perils of Balinese. The spoken language has four different levels, each with its own vocabulary. The level spoken depends on the relative social positions of the speakers, their familiarity with each other, and the social status of the person they are talking about. Social standing is a function of both caste and position within the community; the higher the status, the higher the tongue. As outsiders, we were honored guests, but had neither caste nor position. Wayan felt it appropriate for us to learn one of the higher forms, though that would leave us "above" Darta's family with whom we wished to become more familiar. The complicated solution was to begin studying everything at once. I folded the pages of my notebook into four vertical columns, one for each of the three most common levels of Balinese, and another for Indonesian equivalents. The accumulation of vocabulary was at times painstaking and at others a joy. One day we studied insect names and rushed through three pages of notes in less than an hour, including nearly a dozen words for different kinds of ants. We had never seen Wayan so animated. After sunset, sitting in Suda's kitchen with Pung, we reviewed our notes and learned a few recipes.

"Bees," said Pung. "Boiled in a tasty soup. Seasoned with lemon and onion, and garlic and chili peppers fried in coconut oil. Coconut milk also makes it delicious."

Or, "Wasps. Only certain kinds can be caught; those whose nests have few holes. At night, plug the holes with cotton wool. Cut the nest from where it's hanging. Put it in a bucket and cover it with boiling water. After they're cooked, the wasps taste as good as any other grub. But you have to be careful not to open the nest when you take it down, otherwise you'll wake the wasps and they'll come after you. Also you have to wait for the right month. If you don't, you'll go through all that work only to find the nest empty!"

He went on to talk about grasshoppers, dragonflies, and frogs: how to catch them, and how to eat them.

"*Dongkang*," said Pung. We repeated the new word after him and asked what kind of frog it was. "More bumpy skin," he said. A toad.

"Any more?" I asked.

"There is *emplegan*. Thin with a loud sound. And *ngung*. Same as *emplegan*, but with a pouch for his wind, and louder."

We wrote this all down. Pung went on to describe a *katak*, which appeared to be a bullfrog, and a *godogan*, which he said was a *katak gedé*, a big bullfrog.

"Listen," he said. "They're all out in the paddy tonight." The field sounded like a town full of ringing telephones. "You can't hear those four different sounds?" he asked. We felt a little stupid, but we were happy that the water was still clean enough to support so many fragile amphibians.

As days begot weeks and weeks piled up to form months, we pursued distant glimmering insights into the parallel enigmas of the Balinese language and the workings of a Balinese builder's mind. The kitchen continued to be the focus of many of our learnings. When we pointed out to Nyoman that the kitchen's north wall was a foot longer than the south wall, he assumed we wanted it fixed. He did this by angling the room's front door across the room's northeast corner so that the offending wall was brought down to size. Nyoman was very pleased with his solution. We asked him to redo it.

Communications over the lengths of the kitchen walls were further complicated by a rising controversy over the placement of the room's back door which, in our original drawings, was opposite the front door. When bricks were first laid, space for the back door was left in the wrong corner. We assumed there had been another mistake and gently pointed it out. The next day the crew was erecting the frame in the same spot, and again we talked it through with them. Finally, when the frame was thoroughly bricked and cemented in place, we wondered if the misunderstanding might be cultural. We changed tack from "Don't put the door here" to "Why did you put the door here?" The answer was clear, understandable, and everyone wished that someone had thought of talking about it earlier. They could not build the door where we had asked them to because it would have stood directly in line with the room's front door. Good luck coming into one of the most important rooms in the house would then have gone straight out again.

After that, the kitchen counters became the issue of the day. Having carefully designed his-and-hers counters of wildly differing heights, workmanship made a mockery of all our planning. Sturdy legs were built to support the six-inch-thick, reinforced concrete slabs that were poured as the countertops. Given that the legs started out a little too tall, and that the slabs were thicker than promised, the overall effect was already oversized even before the tilers arrived. They then added another two inches of cement as a bed for the tiles, and did such a poor job that it all had to be ripped out. Adding yet another couple of inches of cement in which to re-lay their work made the countertops gargantuan. For fear of the solution that might be conjured, we dared not point out that the problems they were experiencing in keeping their work true were due to the lack of squareness of their walls.

Work on the second floor and the roofing went smoothly,

however, both being recognizable variations on traditional themes. Once the rat's maze of the downstairs walls was complete, the crew was happy to add what amounted to a regular pavilion as the second story. This part of the construction was a joy. The builders were able to practice their traditional carpentry skills without interference, and Jean and I came to understand how talented they really were. The framing came together confidently and accurately; the grass thatch was laid with speed and in good humor. We began to see that almost everything about our design for the downstairs had been unintelligible to them. If you prepare food on a wooden block while squatting on the floor, why would you think kitchen counters to be of any importance? When you live outdoors and only go inside to close your eyes and sleep, what sense do picture windows make? When all you have to guide you is a confusing drawing, of course you build the kitchen's north wall exactly to specifications!

We congratulated ourselves on our insight and looked forward to a better working relationship through the last weeks of construction. We were fooling ourselves, of course. Understanding past miscommunications and avoiding future misunderstandings are two very different things.

That the cement downstairs floor was laid before we had even met a plumber or an electrician, and that the foundations beneath them were filled with the best loamy topsoil from the garden seemed to be manifold follies: "One, they'll have to dig it all up again to run the utilities. Two, the floors will crack and sink as the soil settles. And three, how will the garden grow?" We came to our wits end when the walls were first beautifully plastered, and then hacked apart to make channels for the plumbing and wiring. When we noticed that the river-rock wall around the shower was a few inches thicker at the top than the bottom we thought of earthquakes and maimed bodies and had it redone. With the pipes exposed, we discovered that the "expert" plumber had put both the cold and hot water taps on the same pipe. There was no hot water piping at all.

By this point two more months had passed and we were nearing hysteria. It was time to go to Singapore again to renew our visas, and we were glad for the break. It was August, and the external structure was complete. The wood mill in Batubulan was still broken and our second floor remained all joists and no floorboards. Work on digging the septic tank, scheduled for "tomorrow" for over a month, had still not begun. And we were not yet satisfied with the quality of the tiling on the bathroom counter. There were a hundred other little jobs to be done before we could move in, but Nyoman claimed he would be done by *Galungan*, an upcoming major Balinese holiday.

As we packed a bag for our brief visa run, we looked forward to moving in. "*Galungan*. Just two and a half more weeks," we told ourselves.

CHAPTER 12

The Wedding

Our visa run to Singapore was without the drama of the previous trip, but lacked none of the expense. The city's cost and standard of living were approaching Tokyo standards rapidly, and we found ourselves trading the culture shock of our last visit for wallet shock.

In search of cheap entertainment, we spent one of our two afternoons exploring the city's subterranean malls in search of Jean's ice cream. In 1983 her company's recipes had been licensed to Japan's largest dairy company. In 1993 the firm opened an ice-cream parlor in downtown Singapore that featured those products. A friend at the company in Tokyo had sent Jean directions to the store. I was to be granted a taste of Jean's life before I met her. After many forays into the city's consumer labyrinths, we found the right store and tasted the magic elixir. It did indeed put the Toko Oen's offerings to shame. But between air-conditioned interiors and steaming city streets, we caught colds for our troubles. Jean claimed this to be a sign, and made me throw away the directions we had been using. "Let sleeping dogs lie," she said.

Back in Denpasar, Darta met us at the airport.

"Good to be back," said Jean.

"True enough!" added Darta, as if he had been all the way to Singapore with us.

Once at home, he sent for his aunt, a local herbalist. She concocted a paste of various gingers, turmeric and rice flour and pasted it across our foreheads and chests. In the morning our colds were gone, but the sheets were stained yellow like the Turin shroud.

"Don't worry," said Darta. "Suti and I will use them. They'll match my old pillow." He was in high spirits, almost too happy. It was clear that all was not well in the household. Somewhere above the kitchen, where the women were cooking, a storm was brewing. By mid-morning the inclement weather had spread right across the compound and grown a dark thunderhead. At lunch time we found Darta sheltering on the steps of the Eastern Pavilion staring at a bush. Thunder and lightning crackled around the compound, and Ibu had become a fire-spitting, cackling old witch. She sat next to Wetni, dressing her up one side and down the other. Wetni was little more than a pool of tears. We were on our way out to find some food. It would have been more polite to leave, but we sat with Darta instead.

"What on earth's going on?" Jean asked.

"Wetni's pregnant." You could have knocked us both over with the same feather. Darta did not even wait for our next question. "Pung," he added.

I thought about this for a moment. A Balinese bride is often pregnant when she gets married. I have even heard people say there would be no reason to wed unless the bride were with child. Pung and Wet had been sweethearts for years—wouldn't they just get married? "So what's the problem," I asked. "There'll be a wedding and that'll be that."

"Yes. If Pung ever asks for her. She's in her fifth month and they haven't said anything to anyone yet."

"You've known all along?" said Jean.

"The women have. They know each other's cycles. They know as soon as one of them misses a mense."

"But you only just found out this morning." It was a guess, but I was right.

"From listening to this!" said Darta. I wondered if he was more upset with Wetni or with his wife and mother for not telling him. "I don't know why this has waited until today."

"I still don't see what the problem is. Is it because Wet isn't pulling her weight with the housework?"

"No." Darta almost laughed at that. "It's the friends and neighbors. They're getting to know. And they're starting to talk. Some are wondering who the father is because he hasn't come forward yet."

"Oh dear," I said. "A scandal. Just like your friend's servant."

"Hmm," said Darta.

"Oh, Pung," sighed Jean.

"So why doesn't Wetni talk to you all now instead of just crying?" I said.

"She can't say anything until Pung does," said Darta. "That's the custom."

"That's a bit rough on Wet!"

"Ibu's frustrated."

"So why doesn't she talk to Pung?"

"None of us are really able to say anything until Pung talks to us all formally."

"Do you think he's going to?"

"He'll have to now."

Ibu's outburst had not been solely a fit of temper. She had let things ride as long as she could. In two weeks the ten-day celebration between the *Galungan* and *Kuningan* holidays would begin. Weddings did not occur during or immediately after this time, and in another five or six weeks the whole village would be talking about Wetni's unmarried condition. Something had to happen. Two weeks was barely enough time, but Ibu had finally gotten the ball rolling.

"My little Pung," said Jean into her rice at the restaurant. "What's he doing?"

"This makes a lot of sense of that conversation you two had about Wetni, doesn't it?"

"Why hasn't he been talking to anybody? Why didn't he say anything to me? We could have worked this out."

"Is it really such a big problem, Jean? Won't it just blow away once he talks to them?"

"I hope so. But I feel hurt that he didn't talk to me. Darta and

Suda have taken him in like a brother. They must really feel betrayed."

"Well, he's not a child anymore. One way or the other, this will make a man out of him."

"Don't be so harsh. He's our little brother and he needs help. I'm going to have to talk to him—get this all straightened out before some irreparable damage is done."

"It's that serious?"

"It easily could be. This isn't just about friendship anymore. It's about social responsibility. If the rules are pushed too far, they'll break. Then everyone will be obliged to break from him and Wet, too."

"Seeing as it's all so delicate, can you really talk to him?"

"I think I'm the only one who still can! The rules don't apply to us. We can go wherever we want and talk to whomever we please. This is our role with this family. Now we get to help them where they can't help themselves—give something in return for all they have done for us."

Pung skulked into the house just before sunset. We had expected fireworks the next time he showed his face, but he was met with polite smiles draped over a stern and expectant silence.

"Pung!" Jean called from our porch. Once she had caught his attention, she waved for him to come back. As Pung walked back up the path to our room, we saw his step had lost all of its usual spring. "How are you?" Jean asked as he sat down on the front step.

"Fine!" Pung's smile was broad and his voice was merry. He began talking about the details of his day, telling us things so ordinary they were hardly worth mentioning. He was clearly straining to cover his deeper emotions. Jean let him go on with his tale.

"Pung," she said gently, and not without a weight of sadness. "Have you seen Wet since lunch time?"

"Yes." The facade evaporated. The boundaries of the conversation were reset. Pung's face began to show the depth of the turmoil he was experiencing.

"Why didn't you say anything?" There was no sense of accusation in her question.

"I was scared."

"This should be so joyous. And suddenly there's so much hurt."

"I've left it too long."

"I know."

"Every day that goes by I get more embarrassed to say anything. I know how angry they're going to be with me."

"Why did you leave it so long?"

"I know Darta, Suti and Ibu. They think I'm too young to get married. I have chances to go abroad, to travel, and get a good job. They think having a child will mean losing all of that because I'll have to stay at home. They would have wanted us to wait. They would have made Wetni have an abortion."

"And you believe the baby is your mother, don't you?" said Jean.

Pung looked at Jean. His gaze was direct and open. Jean took his hand and held it tight, and Pung looked away. People did not do this in Bali. A man would accept comfort from another man, but not from a woman other than his mother, girlfriend or wife. Pung stared into the garden and there were tears in his eyes, but he did not withdraw his hand.

"They're going to be angry with you, and they have a right to be. You've manipulated them and have not been honest with a family that has taken you in as their own. You must listen to what they have to say. But then there will be a wedding and it will all be forgotten. You know that." Pung nodded, but still didn't turn back. "As soon as the baby is born, all their bad feelings will disappear and they'll be fighting to hold the little one. But now you have to go up there and call them all together and ask for Wetni. You were man enough to make the baby, now you must be man enough to take Wetni as your wife." It would have been pointless to have embroidered the words with cultural niceties, and that may well have compromised their power to move him. "It'll be all right. Talk to them tonight."

Pung turned back to her then. "Jean..." He started saying

something, and then stopped. He couldn't quite find the words to thank her for the kick in the backside he knew he had needed, but there was gratitude in his manner. Pung withdrew his hand at last and stood to leave. "I'm going back to my village in the morning. My father will be here at the end of the week," he said before walking away.

"Good," Jean said to his receding shadow. "He'll be coming to make wedding arrangements." Unable to find the courage within himself, Pung was forcing his own hand.

The next evening we came in to find Pung sitting before the assembled elders of the family on the porch of the Western Pavilion. He was alone with them, since Wetni was still at work. It was dark in the rest of the compound. The local power had failed again. Pung sat on one side of a candle. The light shining upward into his face threw his shadow boldly across the garden foliage. Ibu, Darta, Suti, Kadek, Suda, and Paman sat on the other side. Their combined shadows on the pavilion wall resembled the imposing ridges of a high mountain range.

Pung was speaking quietly, but distinctly. His manner was polite. His language was formal. The family members hung on his every word, nodding in agreement at appropriate intervals. It was hard to hear exactly what was being said, so it was unclear to us how long the meeting had been going on. It would have been intrusive of us to emerge from our shadows by the kitchen for a closer view. We watched only long enough to note that Pung's body language was not that of a nervous wreck, and that the family's faces and manner were in harmony and not at odds with the thread of his speech.

It turned out that Pung's request for Wetni's hand in marriage had a number of little stings in its tail. According to tradition in his village, his entire family had to be present at the bride's house for a formal engagement. Pung had been embarrassed to bring this up and had only done so at the end of the conversation. His family was defined as all relatives up to and including first cousins. In practice, this would mean anyone from his village with a yen to see the lights of Ubud. Perhaps as many as a hundred people, for whom the family would be obliged to provide both a meal and an unending stream of coffee, tea, cakes, and cigarettes, would turn up on the doorstep in five days. As the prospective workhorses in such an arrangement, Ibu and Suti were less than enthusiastic. As the financier of such an undertaking, Darta barely concealed his distaste.

None of this was ever spoken of directly. The family would honor the traditions of another village or part of the island with the same level of respect they would expect to be granted to their own customs. The real problem emerged with respect to the date of the ceremony.

The Ubud family wanted things to progress as quickly as possible to quell the local chatter regarding Wetni's pregnancy. In Pung's village, where women seemed to produce children more frequently and from an earlier age, concerns regarding the size of Wetni's belly ran a very poor second to the desire for a highly auspicious day for the wedding. The restrictions and taboos surrounding Pung's father's role as one of the village priests further muddied the waters. The date he wished to propose did not fall until a clear two weeks after *Kuningan*, more than six weeks away. Such an arrangement was completely beyond Ibu's consideration. It did not even bring into question her powers of tolerance. The priest's choice of wedding day was seen not as an issue of tradition as much as one of personal preference. That the wedding could not occur during *Galungan* was accepted without question by all concerned. That one of the two or three reasonably acceptable days before *Galungan* could not be used was regarded by the family as evidence of religious snobbery.

Pung went scampering home the next morning to ask his father for a more acceptable proposal. The priest frowned deeply at the request, but set about rustling through his books. According to his interpretation, there was an all-purpose, any-kind-of-ceremony-that-just-has-to-be-done-before-*Galungan* day that he would consider offering at the formal engagement. Everyone back at the house in Ubud waited with as much bated breath as can be mustered while cooking for a hundred guests.

In the end, a little over a hundred and twenty people arrived. They came mostly by truck, standing shoulder-to-shoulder with the wind in their hair. Some came by chartered minibus. Pung and Rudy took the family car and rented a bus to carry Pung's immediate relations in relative comfort.

Being known to a number of Pung's family, Jean and I were commandeered as back-up hosts and entertainers. In a tangential capacity we were to assist the kitchen. Darta summed up our role by saying, "The more they talk and laugh, the less they'll eat!" We were to circulate and smile. The food and the thermoses and drums of hot water were all prepared by midday, ready for an earliest possible arrival time of one o'clock. It was well after three when the road outside turned into a jam of cars, trucks, buses, and traditionally-dressed bodies. It took a further ten minutes for everyone to file into the compound. They covered every square inch of porch tile and every yard of pavilion step with buttock-to-buttock batik.

The only space where even mildly animated conversation was possible was on the Western Pavilion porch, across the small open area between Paman and Pung's father. Close relatives of both sides squashed in all around them leaving just enough space to put down a cup of coffee and a plate of cakes while the serious business of the event was transacted.

Paman, as Wetni's actual father, conducted the proceedings with a degree of pomp and solemnity I had not expected from his simple farming soul. Since most of the guests were much more interested in eating than talking, Jean and I were able to listen in and cobble together translations for each other. Paman began with a long eulogy regarding his prospective son-in-law. Proving that some clichés are universal and can transcend all cultural barriers, he waxed lyrical for more than fifteen minutes about the delights of gaining a new son. When it came to talk of Wetni, his tone changed markedly. He all but thanked Pung's father for taking such a worthless, no-good, sniveling little wench off his hands. As the host, Paman was expected to be deprecatory of himself and his family, but it was still remarkable to listen to. We doubted what we were hearing more than once, especially knowing how much he loved his daughter.

When it was the priest's turn to speak, he made only passing references to Wetni and focused on the importance of properly joining two families together. It seemed that he was preparing the ground for a post-*Galungan* wedding day proposal, despite all the behind-the-scenes negotiations. In the end, he did offer such a date, but spoke of it in the same breath with which he mentioned a second, though obviously inferior, pre-*Galungan* date.

Ibu and Darta were visibly ruffled by the priest's brinkmanship. Paman, whose thoughts were always practical before being political, made a simple statement invoking common sense to justify choosing the earlier date. There was nothing further Pung's father could say. Talk went on to discuss the details of the impending nuptials.

The wedding itself was something of an anti-climax after all the invested emotion. The less-than-completely-auspicious date for the wedding produced a truncated and less-than-lavish ceremony. Neither Pung nor Wetni seemed to mind the lack of fuss; their primary wish had always been simply to ensure that they got married. But then, even at the best of times, a Balinese wedding ceremony is rarely a matter of romance. The deeper emotions are usually kept for the quiet corners lovers choose for the spinning of their mysteries. There is little public expression of feeling, assuming, of course, that the bride is not too blatantly with child.

The ceremony began with a couple of cars running up to Paman's former home in Junjungan so that Wetni could say goodbye to the deified ancestors enshrined in her family temple. No more than twenty people went on to Pung's home to witness the blessings and the prayers, the offerings to both the high and low spirits, and the introduction of Wetni to the ancestors represented in the groom's ancestral temple.

Jean and I followed in a car with a couple of other guests staying at Darta's. We told them we would leave mid-morning, but they pressed us for a more exact departure time. Making a guess, we told them eleven o'clock. They had not been ready a moment sooner, even though the wedding party had finished their trip to Junjungan with surprising promptness and been on the road before ten. After all that had transpired, we caught only the last five minutes of the ritual, just in time to congratulate the bride and groom. We asked Suti what we should say in Balinese to the newlyweds. She thought about it for a moment and then told us there was no specific phrase she could teach us. "We just turn up and smile a lot," she said.

CHAPTER 13

Galungan

Galungan falls on the Wednesday of the eleventh week of the two-hundred-and-ten-day Balinese calendar. The full celebration runs for ten days through *Kuningan*, the Saturday of the following week. During this time the deified ancestors are said to return home to visit their living descendants. Schools are closed, and all commercial and local government activity grinds to a halt.

For the three days prior to *Galungan* itself, preparations are at their most intensive and are accompanied by the arrival of disruptive spirits. It is a time for minding one's temper and guarding against angry exchanges or fights with family members. On the first of these days, bananas are picked or bought so that they will be ripe for *Galungan*. *Tapé*, a mildly alcoholic fermented rice pudding, is also prepared. The next day is spent in the making of cakes. Darta describes this day as "an inspiration! Everyone is happy and tries to eat the cakes as soon as they are made. It makes us all look forward to and think seriously about *Galungan*."

The day before *Galungan* is called *Penampahan*, which means "to slaughter an animal." The morning is spent butchering pigs. The meat is finely minced and then either mixed into an assortment of fiery dishes, known as *lawar*, or wrapped around the end of thick skewers and barbecued as *saté*. This is also the last day to erect the tall, highly decorated bamboo poles called *penjors* that stand outside each front gate. Every street becomes an arching avenue of lacy fronds, setting up the whole island for a great party.

As vegetarians, *Penampahan* Eve was hard to sleep through. The whole process began at the stroke of midnight. All around, from every pig pen in the back of every nearby household, came the squealing of terrified porkers. In walking the village we may not have come to know each animal as a personal friend, but by sense of smell alone we had at least come to develop a nodding acquaintance. The screaming ended at about 4 a.m., once the last pig had been caught and had its snout bound.

Though often invited to help with the buthering, I had always declined. I once saw Suda fillet a dozen fish he had been nurturing in the pond in front of his house. He didn't even knock them on the head; it was exactly like being back in a Japanese sushi bar. To see a friend perform the same act on a large mammal would have been more than I could stomach.

In the morning, dear Darta, ever sensitive to our moods, sympathized with our feelings. "You know I'm starting to become a vegetarian, too," he said. "When we kill pigs or ducks I never eat the insides anymore. I don't eat the organs, only the meat. I don't ever eat *lawar* or *saté* made from the offal. I know that the fat is not good for me, and it's clear that I already have enough fat on me to last a long time, so I am eating less meat, half of what I used to."

"You mean half as much?"

"No, half as many different kinds. You know, it's not good to make sudden changes. If I am trying to paint a white wall black, one thick coat will peel off and then be gone. If I apply color thinly and over time, the wall changes slowly from white to black. So it's already certain that I will eventually become a vegetarian, though my colors will change slowly but surely."

My sleep on *Galungan* Eve was fitful for other, more sentimental, reasons. In resonance with the local level of anticipation, I tossed and turned all night like I had as a child on Christmas Eve. An hour before sunrise, as the roosters began to crow, I awoke to the sounds of Suti and Ibu about the kitchen. I heard rice being tossed in a flat, round basket to separate the chaff, and smelled the first wisps of a coconut-husk fire in the kitchen grate.

Next I became aware that people were moving through the family temple, just outside the bedroom door. They made their final preparations by the light of a neon strip bulb that had been specially rigged to show the ancestors the way home and had kept me awake for a good part of the night. I heard Ibu and Suti again, and it sounded like Darta was doing some sweeping. They were close to the guest rooms and their voices were hushed. Having filed the usual sharp edges off of their clattering tongues, their tones were like brass pans falling on soft earth, sweet and lulling.

Even with that, sleep still eluded me. I slipped out of bed, dressed, and wandered out into the compound. I had to see if Darta really was sweeping. I found him out on the front steps with broom in hand, a sight possible only on this one day of the year. He asked me why I had been sleeping in; the whole family had already been down to the river for the traditional *Galungan* morning bath.

By six, the usual preparations for the homestay guests were under way. Fruit salads were being prepared and water was on the boil. A full flask and a change of cups was taken to each porch where any empty jars of coffee, tea or sugar were refilled.

"Where's Wet?" I asked Lolet.

"With Pung," he said.

"Oh, yes." As Pung's wife, she would spend *Galungan* in his village. To make up for her absence, Suti was overseeing the kitchen and helping Ibu with the day's offerings on the Western Pavilion.

"We only do offerings like this three times a Balinese year," she said in passing, "today for *Galungan*, in ten days time for *Kuningan*, and for the family temple anniversary. All this took thirty days to make." Offerings were taken to all the shrines around the compound and within the family temple, to the front step of each building, and to the front gate. There was even an offering on the telephone. "To ensure its health and longevity," Suti assured me.

I had good reason not to doubt the influence of magic over mechanics. The old family car had recently let us down on a trip to east Bali only days after a major mechanical repair. A roadside mechanic got the car going again, but could not say what had been wrong or what he had done to set it right. On the way home Darta remembered he had neglected to have Ibu perform a reanimation ceremony for the car after its first bout of surgery. This omission was seen as the basic problem. Once the offerings were made, the car ran faultlessly.

By the front gate there was a small commotion as Darta unveiled a new bicycle he had just bought for Tutut and Abut. "I told Tutut if she became number one, two or three in her class, I'd get her a new bike," said Darta to me. The children were ecstatic but did not even think of riding the bike until Tutut had put on a sarong and temple scarf and made an offering. A little palm-leaf tray with a holy cargo of blossoms and rice grains, incense, and a woven palm-leaf fan had already been prepared by Suti. Tutut and Abut reverentially tied the fan to the handlebars, lit the incense and laid it on the fan. Tutut then splashed the whole offering with holy water from a glass. Holding a pure white frangipani bloom between the fore and middle fingers of her right hand, she etched three slow counter-clockwise circles through the smoke with both the movement of the flower and the intention of her prayers. I have seen Tutut dance, and in both dance and prayer she wears a charisma that completely defies her tender years. When the dance or the prayer ends, she is immediately a little girl once again. No sooner had the frangipani flower completed its third loop than the sarong and scarf were discarded and brother and sister were out on the street, taking turns to ride.

"I remember when Roda got me a bicycle," said Darta, watching them play. "After coming back from Flores he was stationed in Klungkung, in east Bali. All the children except me were with him and Ibu. I was here with my grandmother, going to school in Ubud. Because she was old and sometimes got sick, there were times when I got home from school and there was no food. I tried not to cry when I was hungry, and if I did, I tried not to let her see. But sometimes she saw me, and I knew she felt bad. Maybe this only happened two or three times, but it made an impression on me. Usually, if she hadn't cooked, she would go to the market and spend what little money she had with the rice seller.

"Na. I went to school with the rice seller's son. We would walk home together, then he would run in and get a plate full of as much food as he wanted. Oh! I was so jealous. My mouth watered, and then I'd get home and there'd be nothing and I'd cry.

"Then one *Galungan*, Roda and the rest of the family came home with two presents for me: a new child's bicycle and a red shirt. Oh! I was so excited. I jumped on the bicycle and went all over town. I even went to school where some students were helping to clean up, just to show off the bike. Many people had bikes then, but there were few of the small bikes a child could ride. I came home all sweaty and it was time to eat. Ibu had brought cakes from Klungkung and it was a feast. I should have bathed before I ate but I was so excited. I just put on my new shirt and started eating. I remember it all vividly. It was the happiest day of my young life.

"After that I rode that bike to school every day. Then it was the rice seller's son's turn to be jealous. He used to give me food in exchange for a ride on the bike. He'd come to school with a whole piece of tofu in his shirt pocket. What a mess! But tofu like that was expensive, and delicious!

"That was my first experience of renting out transportation," he added seriously. "I was ready for the arrival of the tourists from an early age. Also, that new red shirt was the one taken by the boy who ate pens and tables and became a magician. Remember?" I remembered. "Na. We'd have breakfast on *Galungan* morning; our first breakfast for thirty weeks!" Balinese usually only eat an early lunch and then dinner. "Then we'd dress up and go down to the village. We'd just wander around, not knowing where we were going. At the community hall there would be gambling, and in the afternoon someone would try to get a cockfight together. Before noon all the women would have to take offerings to the village temples, to the shrines around the house, and to the houses of relatives where there had been a marriage. They would also go to the cremation ground if there had been a recent death and the body was still waiting for cremation. This was too much work if there was only one woman in the household.

"Every half hour we children would come running home to eat. We weren't really hungry, but our eyes were. All that *lawar* and all those cakes! And then there would be the *barongs* in the street. In

Ubud, all our ceremonies are big now. It's hard to see how special *Galungan* once felt."

Right at that moment, round the corner down the street, came a lion-like *barong* with snapping jaws, wide eyes and a flowing mane. This was not Ubud's holy *barong*, it was a performance piece. With a retinue of crashing cymbals and sonorous gongs the *barong* proceeded up the street, stopping to dance a brief exorcism before each house that offered a few coins. In this way, the neighborhood would be cleared of disturbing spirits for the holiday. The man animating the *barong's* head was being very energetic. His partner working the tail was having a hard time keeping up. The overall effect was one of mangled confusion. In a few paces another pair of men stepped under the costume to take over and began producing a much more harmonious and realistic show.

One of my all-time favorite pictures of Jean was taken on the morning of my first *Galungan* in Bali. When I took it, I was standing across the street from the family house watching the progress of a serious-minded children's *barong* up the street. When they stopped in front of the house I took a picture of the scene. It included Jean, up in the compound, looking over the waist-high front wall, with Ibu and Suti at her side. The members of the orchestra were standing between me and the house, and the prancing *barong* was still off to one side. In the picture Jean is leaning on the wall, looking off toward the *barong*, her chin cupped in her hand. Her face is a picture of delight. Everything about her posture is at ease. Though just a small part in a complex composition, she shines out at me whenever I look at that photograph.

It was already after midday when Suda made his first appearance at the family house. He was grubby and tired and asked for a jug of water.

"Where have you been, getting all hot and sweaty?" I asked.

"Judging *penjors*," he replied. There was a competition for the best one in town and Suda was a judge. He had been trudging all over Ubud to see potential prize winners.

"How do you judge them?" I asked. "How did this house do?"

Suda flashed me a wide grin and shook his head in answer to my last question. He handed me his clipboard and scoring notes for me to figure out my own answer to the former. It appeared that an awful lot more went into the creation of each forty-foot *penjor* than I had thought. Beyond the selection of an elegantly arching piece of bamboo and the weaving of a long streamer to hang from its tip, Suda's form listed a dozen further levels of detail, each of which could be awarded up to ten marks. There were points for the flourish with which the streamer ended, and the intricacy of the snail-shell wind chime. A complete *penjor* also included a string of flowers, bananas and cakes that were tied to the streamer half-way up its length as an offering, and a pair of white and yellow cloths hanging from the top of the *penjor's* arch. Then there was a mark for the level of attention with which the bamboo had been finished. The next section dealt with the small triangular offering-niche that is constructed at about chest level. If it was supported by only one leg, contained the appropriate offerings, and was draped with a long, well-woven and colorfully decorated *lamak* palm-leaf hanging, it scored well. Finally, there were another eighty marks available for each of two categories that were the equivalent of technical merit and artistic impression.

"You're judging all these parts, but what do each of them mean symbolically?"

Suda shrugged. "They all mean something," he said. I don't know if he was just tired or really did not know. "Ask Suti," was his final word on the subject.

"Are you finished with the judging yet?" I asked.

"We've done North Ubud, Sambahan and Central Ubud. Just South Ubud still to do."

Suti wasn't yet back from her village offering-making round, but her husband was willing to venture an opinion about the symbolism of the *penjor* in her absence. "The *penjor* is an offering to show gratitude for everything we get from the earth. All the materials and food we need are represented. It is tall so that all the visiting ancestors and all the gods on Mount Agung can see it. And it honors the great serpent Anantaboga who lives under Mount Agung. Anantaboga means food without end. The *penjor* is made in his shape. Go and look: the offering place at the bottom is his head, the decorations on his arching body are scales, and the wind chime is the tip of his tail."

I went out onto the street again to see for myself, and to listen to the tinkle of little wind chimes in the breeze. I must have been standing there only a few minutes when an extraordinarily loud female voice addressed my back from way down the street. "William," she bellowed. "What are you doing, standing in the middle of the road, staring into space?"

I spun around. "Madé!" I shouted. "I haven't heard you sounding so well since that morning in Solo! And Ardika! Hello, old friend!" Madé and her husband were walking up the way with their three children.

"How did you get here?"

"Public bus. Very crowded," said Ardika.

"How long are you staying?"

"We'll leave early in the morning."

"Great. Come in. Come in. Jean will be so excited to see you." You would have thought it was my family home, not Madé's, the way I was speaking. No offense was meant, and there was certainly none taken.

Madé always made rice cakes for *Galungan*. The moment she walked into the compound she handed a bag of them to the kitchen. They were quickly served up and the kitchen was soon full of people.

"The cakes aren't all I brought," said Madé to everyone. "I got a letter yesterday from Putu."

"Putu?" said Ibu. "What did he say? What did he say?" Her fifth child worked as a policeman on the distant island of Flores.

"Ayun is pregnant and they're coming home," Madé continued. "They'll be here in early December. They'll stay in Ubud, and Putu will work at police headquarters in Denpasar."

The excitement lasted all afternoon and most of the evening. I couldn't help thinking how like Christmas it was: the family was all together, or soon would be, and there was more food than anyone could eat. But even better than Christmas, and closer to all my childhood dreams, it usually came not once, but twice a year.

CHAPTER 14

Monkey Forest Road

Kuningan marked the end of the ten-day celebration that began with *Galungan*. The ancestral spirits left and life got back to normal. We moved out to one of Suda's dark little rooms in the rice field to oversee the final touches to our new house. The builders had taken nearly two weeks off for the holiday, but no sooner had they returned than they announced they would be away in another two weeks for a temple ceremony in their village.

"How long will you be gone this time?" we asked Nyoman.

"Oh, not long. Another week perhaps. But I think we can finish here before that."

Based on what we knew of Nyoman and his crew, this seemed unlikely, but we could hardly begrudge them the time off. The richness of the Balinese ceremonial culture was what made living on the island so palatable.

After the *Galungan* break and with another holiday soon to come, everyone returned to work with renewed vigor. Things were going well for us, we thought, until we got up one morning to find the coiled carcass of a three-foot-long rice field eel on our front porch, right in front of our door. Even though all the temple theft fervor had died way down, gossip about the magic man in the tree, and black magic in general, persisted. Sensitized to these concerns, we immediately concluded that the carefully coiled eel was the work of a jealous neighbor. We heard Darta's and Suda's voices across the rice field. They were up at the front house talking over coffee and we went to seek their advice. They listened carefully as we recounted our tale.

"If there was really anything to worry about, we'd tell you," began Darta. "A dead chicken. A cat. We'd call Ibu and Paman in for that. Offerings would be needed. Some defensive planning would be called for. But believe me when I tell you that no one, no one does black magic using eels!"

"A cat caught it and left it there," said Suda, ever the pragmatist. "And there's a good story about eels, too. You meditate and do a lot of yoga. At night, eels are often seen flying around the houses of people who do things like that."

"We haven't been here even a week," I pointed out, "and they're on the wing already?"

"Maybe," said Suda.

"And this one got a little close and crashed perhaps?"

"What about whatever it is that crashes through the bushes at night back there?" Jean said. "Last night I was woken by all this splashing in the pond. It must have been something very big. But when I went out to look, there was nothing."

"You're thinking it might have been a spirit?" asked Suda.

"Oh! They really are becoming Balinese!" laughed Darta. No further explanation of our "water spirit" was offered. We were simply told not to worry about it. "The moment it starts coming into your room, you tell us, and we'll start making offerings. That's why we have rooms to sleep in with doors that shut and small windows with bars: to keep that kind of thing out."

In truth, we were all wide of the mark. Months later we found out that the water spirit, the black magician, and what we had assumed to be a nightly game of cat and mouse above the false ceiling in our little room were all manifestations of an *alu*, a three-foot long, twelve-pound monitor lizard living in the roof. She was eventually discovered when Pung had to replace a number of tiles she had broken on her way in and out. He got hold of her tail and held on while calling for help. She put up a hell of a fight, but Pung and his friends finally caught her. We asked that she be released in a nearby river, but someone got hold of her and put her in a pen. *Alu* oil is considered a strong medicine for serious burns; the lizard would be kept for just such an emergency, then boiled down for the oil. We were appalled. But then the same quality of workmanship that had been applied to parts of our house was used in the construction of the *alu's* pen, and she escaped in the middle of her first night of captivity.

While her indomitable presence in our rafters was still a fresh mystery, however, another, far more emotive kind of horror struck Ubud. Jean and I were walking through town toward the market and crossing the end of Monkey Forest Road. The Monkey Forest itself was a tiny remnant of the virgin forest that once must have covered most of central Bali. Within its shade lays Padangtegal's Temple of the Dead and the village's cremation ground. Among its trees live a troupe of monkeys who make their living from intimidating tourists shipped in by the busload for their pleasure. Between this wood and the main crossroads of Ubud ran a road lined with hotels, souvenir shops, restaurants, and beautiful shade trees. Crossing the end of the street that day was like arriving home and sensing that the furniture has subtly been rearranged: you know something is wrong but it takes a few moments for it to dawn on you that you have been carefully and systematically robbed.

"The trees," said Jean flatly. "They've all been cut down."

When we got home we confronted Suda with what his village had done.

"Who'll want to walk down that street in the heat of the day without shade?" we railed. "The tourist buses are already too big for the roads. You should be stopping the buses, not cutting down the trees to widen the roads. You wait and see. It's just a matter of time before a tourist is hit and killed. People will stop going down there and then where will your profits be? You keep going on about progress but none of you think it through! It's not just on Monkey Forest Road either. This village used to be full of tall trees, and it was cool to walk out among them. Now look at it. We've made mistakes in our countries; we've already damaged our environments. Why haven't you learned from our mistakes? Don't just copy them blindly!"

"Now, you listen to me!" Suda contended. "The decision to cut those trees was made at a village level. We thought it through and decided it was best. You come here for just a few months a year, but you know almost nothing about how things work here. How often are you stuck in traffic jams trying to get through Ubud on market day? If you don't like it, you can leave. Go home! We've had white people telling us what to do in Indonesia for four hundred years. Now we're independent. Now we are free to make our own decisions. I've heard you say television is bad, that the advertising is wrecking our culture's values and turning our children's minds, but you watched it for twenty years! How dare you say that I can't! When I was in California with you, Jean, we went to see the big redwood trees, and you told me how they used to be everywhere near the ocean but now there are only a few pockets left. You cut them all down! Maybe we are making mistakes. Of course we will make mistakes. All humans do. But at least we're making our own mistakes, and enjoying our own successes! You know, if I could go back to life before tourists," Suda slapped his hand on the arm of his chair, "I'd do it in an instant!"

Raw nerves had been touched all round. The whole event made a mess of everyone's day. The fire was hot and bright but, true to form, it was short-lived. The very next day we were sitting with Suda and Kadek, talking things over much more soberly.

"We all lost our tempers yesterday," said Suda, "and, you know, we got in a lot of trouble over felling those trees. Some very big tour companies complained that Monkey Forest Road will get too hot and dangerous. It was on TV and in the newspapers."

I had to admire his magnanimity. "Would you like to see some kind of meeting between Balinese and foreigners?" I asked. "So we can all share what we know?"

"No, I don't think so," said Suda. "The foreigners don't make any problems, so there isn't any need to meet with them."

So many messages in such a short sentence: We had not been included in the "them," which was nice, but neither was there room left in which to have much of a say. Suda had never intended it as such, but Jean and I felt very much put in our place.

"Do foreigners join the *banjar* village councils?" I asked.

"Yes, if they own land here, they can join." The whole tone of Suda's conversation made it clear that he saw the cross-cultural mechanism as already existing in the form of the village community organization. "It works. Why set up anything else?" seemed to be his attitude. Also, we were asking for a voice he did not see us as deserving. Rights, within the village system are not inalienable. They are commensurate with the degree to which you fulfill your responsibilities. If you do not answer the *kulkul* bell when it sounds for work at the temple or in the ditch beside the street, you lose your vote at the next bi-weekly village meeting. The richer you are, the deeper your obligation to share what you have through contributions to the community. With the power to control resources comes a commensurate responsibility to one's environment and society. If you don't fulfill your responsibilities, you are shunned. In the West we have lost many of the mechanisms that should control those who wield the most power. Within the Balinese village, the checks function very simply.

There was a very rich and arrogant Brahmana in a nearby village who never contributed to the community and whom nobody liked. When he died, nobody came to help with the funeral rites. Something in the stars made it necessary to perform an immediate and elaborate cremation, so the family had to spend thousands of dollars hiring the people of another village while the locals sat around and watched. For a Balinese, guaranteeing that your cremation is performed correctly and your soul is released properly are of the utmost importance, so this sanction has real power. However, ostracism can be enforced in far less dramatic ways for less serious infringements of etiquette: just being missed off the list of invitations to a wedding can be a serious embarrassment. In practice, flapping tongues do a great deal of the community policing.

Certainly our presence at the local temple ceremonies was noticed and appreciated, but that level of respect did not amount to a whole lot of influence. Our state of relating to the culture through a family without plugging formally into the community felt nebulous.

"Suda, do you think we fulfill our responsibilities to this community?" I asked.

"I don't think that's a reasonable question," he said. "This is not your country or your community. If you can think in terms of this family you will feel better. We listen to you. You may feel that we're just humoring you, but we think about what you say and talk about what you think. Knowing you has helped us a lot."

"Do you know any foreigners who've lived here for a long time and keep close Balinese friends?" Jean asked.

Both Suda and Kadek said they did not. "Tourists who visit stay close with us, they come again and again. People who live here don't seem to do that," said Suda.

"Unless they marry a Balinese and have children here," added Kadek.

Neither of their answers was reassuring. We went on to talk about the pitfalls of being from cultures on flip sides of history's colonial coin, and how the habitual attitudes of the colonizer and the colonized can get in the way. Suda spoke of how proud he was to be Balinese. Jean talked about how Suda would fall asleep when she and Eric talked about their relationships with their home nations and how they had struggled to find a sense of "home."

Jean's comment made me think of Pung's younger sister Ketut. She had recently come down from their village to stay at Suda's and go to school. When she first arrived, nobody mothered her. There was no welcome, and there was no special attention to ease her transition. She accepted the situation without tears or complaint. That she might feel lost or insecure never occurred to anyone, including her brother. She was expected to find her place and assumed to posses a degree of selfhood that would have been considered remarkable in the West. In short, the Balinese had no experience from which to relate to our lost sense of place. And a lost sense of place was what we realized we were experiencing.

"We left Japan not knowing where we were going," said Jean, "and we've been away from our own countries for so long that we don't know if we belong there anymore either. So there is a feeling of being lost. But I've always thought of Bali as a kind of paradise, a place removed from the troubles of the world, a haven. I guess the events of the last months have proved me wrong."

"Bali doesn't have the answer, does it?" I said later, when Jean and I were alone.

"No. But part of the answer is here: community and spirituality are where you begin."

A local trance-medium we once met told us how important the climbing of mountains was to the pursuit of inner peace. Remembering this, Jean decided that a little spiritual refreshment was in order. As the workers prepared to return home for their temple ceremony, she suggested that we use the opportunity to go to Pung's village. "What if we climb Mount Batukau?" she said.

CHAPTER 15

The Road to Nowhere

Pung, Jean and I left Ubud early in the morning. Rudy drove us across Bali to the hamlet where Pung had grown up. Since the time of his mother's death, the path to the village had been widened. Motor vehicles could negotiate the rutted lane, but only in the dry season. The village itself was unchanged. Forty-three compounds lined a single street along the spine of a narrow ridge among fertile rice fields. The land sloped upwards towards the line of mountains that divide central and western Bali. Batukau was the tallest of these peaks, and the second highest mountain on the island. Our plan was to spend a day on the climb, spend the night at the temple on the summit, and take another day for the descent. Joining us were Pung's brother Ketut and his cousin Wayan. We met them both in Pung's family compound. We visited just long enough to be polite, but it was still after midday by the time food, clothing and the required offerings had been organized and shared out among the packs. Rudy drove us back out of the village and up to the trail head at the foot of the mountain. As we waved good-bye, it began to rain. It was nearly three o'clock.

"Only two hours to the top," said Pung. "Don't worry." Unable to resist the magic of his Puck-like grin, we turned our backs on civilization and common sense, and started trudging uphill. The track was wide and much-traveled as far as a complex of five temples dedicated to various deities of the Balinese-Hindu pantheon. We stopped briefly at the gate of the first where Wayan laid an offering and incense on the temple steps and whispered a prayer for our safe passage. Beyond the temples, a narrow foot-path wound upward through woodland gardens. The rain had stopped, Ketut and Wayan were out ahead, and Pung was singing an Indonesian children's song:

The bird I call Older Brother
Sits at the window.
My grandmother who is really old
Has only two teeth.

We passed a sign marking the boundary of a National Forest and the path steepened. Signs of cultivation vanished and we were left with just the voice of the rain forest. Birdsong drifted through the trees on a stiff breeze, and Pung had a name to go with every call. We found ourselves on a ridge trail with the sound of running water far below us. As we climbed, the sound grew stronger. It seemed we would soon come upon a sizable waterfall. Instead we encountered a blustery squall. As it rose up out of the foothills and crested the ridge, the only thing Ketut had to say was, "*Hujan.*" Rain. He was not a man of many words.

The rain passed quickly, and after another hour we came to a small spring. "We'll rest here awhile," said Pung. "This place is sacred." Wayan lit another stick of incense and went down to the water's edge to make a second offering. "Wayan says we are already halfway to the top. You can trust him. He's climbed this mountain three times before."

An hour and a half later, the six of us sat silently looking out through a space in the canopy at clouds painted crimson by the departing sun.

"How much farther now, Wayan?" we asked.

"Half an hour," he said, "maybe twenty-five minutes."

After that brief reststop the squalls became more frequent and the trail degenerated into a greasy scramble. Making no conces-sions to circumstance, the path just went straight up. We struggled on, making handholds of tree trunks and footholds among roots. As dusk gathered among the trees, we broke out our two flash-lights. Ketut and Wayan took one; Jean, Pung and I shared the other. Where the path was clear, we could walk close together, sharing a small circle of light. During frequent moments of difficulty, the one with the flashlight would make a pitch of a few yards before turning to throw an umbilical cord of light back to the other two.

"Wayan. Wayan! Are we close?" Pung was just up ahead, holding the light for us and shouting to his cousin. There was a note of panic in his voice.

"Yeah, yeah." The words came back to us out of the night.

The rain became constant and soaked us to the skin. The wind was sharp and chilling. By flashlight, we scuttled across narrow ledges around rocky outcrops, clambered over fallen logs, crashed through rhododendron forests booby-trapped with barbed vines, and flicked little inch-worm leeches from our arms and legs. Each of us met and had to deal with our private terrors: a night out in the rain, the fear of falling, the ignominy of dying of hypothermia on a tropical island. Wayan and Ketut were by now way ahead, far beyond earshot.

"Are we still on the trail, Pung?" asked Jean.

"Yes," he replied. "I think so."

"Just keep going up," said Jean. "This mountain has to have a top. Ketut and Wayan are probably waiting for us at the temple with a meal ready and a fire blazing."

At nine o'clock the rain stopped and the three of us changed out of our wet clothes. Pung gave us each a rice ball. We ate together in silence until the party was abruptly ended by another squall. We changed back into our wet clothes and continued our forced march. We stopped talking and wouldn't look into each other's faces for fear of the fatigue we would see. For another hour the trail continued upwards. Then suddenly, inexplicably, the trees stood back from the path, the ground leveled out, and above us opened a vast, star speckled night. "It's the top," said Jean, bewildered. "And it's not raining!" Just ahead, a billowing cloud of smoke announced Wayan and Ketut's warm welcome.

"The temple pavilions are too small up here for us all to sleep in," said Wayan apologetically. "This fire pit is the only place we have." The pit was square and ten feet on a side with a shaky corrugated iron roof. Wayan was squatting by a tiny pile of firewood, surrounded by ash, with his hands full of damp kindling. Ketut was prostrated beside the fire, his face almost in the ashes, blowing gently on a tiny ember. "A prayer to Brahma, god of the kitchen fire," joked Wayan. Reluctant to ignore such an invocation, the fire sprang into life once more and continued to billow blinding smoke.

Sitting upwind of the fire, and most of its heat, we changed into our dry clothing. "They've brought all the warm clothes they own and it's still not enough," said Jean. She lent Pung a pair of silk leggings, which he wore with a pair of shorts and his jacket. Ketut wore a denim jacket already wet from the climb and a pair of jeans rolled up three times at the ankles. Wayan put on my second sweater and a pair of my shorts that came down to his calves.

Before we could eat, Wayan went out with a rice ball and incense to pray at the temple altar. When he returned we tucked into the food we had carried up from the village: spicy vegetables, fried eggs, soybean cake and rice balls, served on banana-leaf plates. We ate slowly, savoring the moment. The prospects for sleep did not seem good, so we avoided the issue for as long as possible. After dinner we all wandered off in our separate directions to improvise a toilet. Emerging from behind my bush, I found myself looking out across the lights of southern Bali. There wasn't a cloud in sight and planes on final approach to Denpasar glided by below me. Above, the Milky Way seemed close enough to step onto.

Pung came up and stood beside me. "In Bali we believe the Milky Way is the road the dead take to heaven."

"It's still quite a way above us, so I guess we're not ready for it yet then," I said. "Got to spend a little time in the grave first. C'mon. Let's go lie down in the ashes."

Getting our motley crew to bed was not easy. We let the fire go out and built a windbreak out of some sheets of corrugated iron Jean had discovered on her bathroom trip. Then we tackled the problem of getting five people into two sleeping bags. Jean and I fought with the tube bag for five minutes before concluding that two large Westerners could not use it. We gave it to Wayan and Ketut to see if two small Balinese could share it. Wayan, the smallest in the group, took it, thanked us, jumped in and fell into a death-like sleep. That left four of us to share the remaining bag, which unzipped into a double blanket. Even some very intimate spooning left Jean on one end and Pung on the other half exposed to the elements, but at least they had room to move. Ketut and I, like yogis on beds of nails, had to eke out some semblance of equanimity among the sharp stones with which we were to spend the night. Life became something of a meditation: a lot more zazen than zzz.

Being essentially paralyzed by my situation, and yet acutely aware of my aching body, I was completely unable to sleep. I tried counting my breaths, but this made me too aware of the flints between my ribs. I tried counting Jean's breaths, but that didn't help much either, so I took to moon-gazing. A piercingly bright gibbous moon stood in the middle of my field of vision. I remembered that the full moon was three nights away, and figured out that the moon would therefore set around three o'clock. "It'll then be three more hours to sunrise," I thought, unsure if this was a consoling notion or not.

I looked out over my feet and away from the moon. The altitude and the lack of city lights meant that thousands of stars were out. A starry sky always fills me with a sense of awe. Intergalactic distances make me feel small and comfortably insignificant. I stared into the night, and thought about the mountain we were on, and the Balinese belief that it was alive with a great, intelligent spirit. I looked at the universe before me and it too seemed to be overflowing with an all-pervasive genius. It suddenly seemed very strange that I, an almost infinitesimally small participant in the cosmic drama, should consider myself and my species separate from the activity of this spirit. Wasn't it obvious that our impact on the planet, and the feeling I had that we should mend our ways, were both guided by this greater intelligence?

I listened as rain fell on the forest below the summit and was glad of the company and the meager shelter. At least I no longer feared for my life. I even fell into a fitful sleep and dreamed that Jean and I were searching for Pung through the rooms of an

English country house. Eventually we found him in the study, hiding under the desk with John Gielgud.

Meanwhile Jean was dealing with a far more serious situation. She had not wanted to disturb my precious slumber and waited until I awoke again to whisper her story to me. "I heard a scuffling in the bags by my head, and when I opened my eyes I was nose-to-pointy-nose with a large white rodent. His face was full of the fried egg we had planned to have at breakfast. I stared into his beady little eyes and he stared back, both of us aware that one of us was going to bolt, but neither of us certain who it would be. Then you snored, and I remembered that I was a human. He remembered that he was a rat and ran off into the dark."

Once the moon had set, I figured that we should all turn over and offer the left sides of our bodies some of the numbness our right sides were luxuriating in. When we all sat up, Pung was the last to rouse. Somehow he had appropriated enough of the blanket to wrap himself almost completely. He was in no hurry to surrender his prize.

When darkness gave way to the dawn's thin light, Wayan was the first to rise. One by one we followed him out. We looked like a grubby band of lost coal miners. Our clothes and faces were black and we had ash in our hair. But we were on top of the world. The air was perfectly clear. We could see practically forever in every direction. All around us birdsong rose up out of the forest. "Listen!" said Pung. "There are monkeys, too!" To the east, the sun rose over Bali's tallest peak, Mount Agung. Beyond Agung we could see as far as Mount Rinjani, ninety miles away on the island of Lombok. To our left, a number of Bali's smaller peaks peered at their reflections in the still mirror of Lake Bratan. Far beyond the northern coast, a serious-looking group of thunderclouds blustered about, full of their own self-importance. Southward, we looked down upon a sky-blue mosaic of flooded rice fields. To the west we could see deep into Java. We even fancied that we could make out the distant tip of Mount Semeru.

"Is Batukau a volcano?" Jean asked.

Pung shrugged. "Not today."

"I think it must be," I said. "Isn't this whole line of mountains volcanic?" I looked north along the line of peaks. At the end of the range was Lake Tamblingan in its caldera, and Mount Lesung with its forested crater. Local lore stated that both were sleeping. Places with names like Boiling Water and Buried in Ash were said to be reminders of past eruptions.

"The god Shiva," said Pung, "sent seven of his children from Semeru to the sacred places of Bali. Batukau has the oldest temple because the gods coming from the west arrived here first. Before that there was a temple here, but no god."

While the others convened for breakfast, Jean and I pondered Pung's conundrum. "Before Hinduism came here from Java, the Balinese worshipped nature spirits," conjectured Jean. We stood on the very top of the mountain by a small stone altar. A stunted tree was wrapped in the black-and-white checkered cloth by which the Balinese recognize the presence of a powerful spirit. The shrine stood above and separate from the buildings of the temple proper and seemed older. "They had temples, but none of the present gods."

"*Makan*! *Makan*! Let's eat!" called Pung. The coal miners were not a quorum without us, and our vote was required in order to mandate the eating of food. We walked down and squatted with them in a little circle. Wayan handed us each a banana-leaf plate full of food.

"Wayan, what happened the last three times you were up here?" I asked between mouthfuls.

"I first came up here with five friends when I was about eighteen," he replied. "It was very cold. We built a big fire and stayed close to it all night. Another time we came up here to meditate. The weaker ones sat for one or two hours, then went to bed."

"Did you have blankets?" Jean asked. "What did you do?"

"We were like this," said Wayan, hugging his knees and shivering.

We finished our meal by eight o'clock and sat soaking up the heat of the sun's rays. From the main road around Lake Bratan the sounds of traffic drifted up to us on an early thermal. Before beginning our descent, Wayan made one last offering at the shrine on the summit while we gathered our gently steaming clothing from the tin roof of the fire pit.

"How long will it take us to get down?" Jean asked Pung.

"About two hours?" he ventured.

"C'mon," I said. "I just looked at the map. To get here we had to climb four and a half thousand feet and it took us all night. You still say we can get down in two hours?"

"Don't worry. Be happy," was all he had to say in reply.

The way down was breathtakingly beautiful. All those hours we had been slogging up a ridge through an enchanted forest draped with ferns and encrusted with jewel-like mosses. Only by daylight were we able to appreciate it. I pulled my camera out of my pack and snapped off half a roll. In all of the pictures I took that morning our faces are graced with dreamy smiles.

The touch of heaven was short-lived. After two hours, Pung was still saying it would be two hours more. The ridge and its occasional views had given way to steep slopes and heavy woodland. After the previous night's rain, the trail was a mudslide. My knees began to complain more with every step. My sense of happiness slipped away. I became bored, then annoyed, and finally decided I was furious with Pung.

"As a guide, he's misjudged this trek every step of the way," I said to Jean. "If it's going to take six hours he should be honest with us. He's betrayed the trust we placed in him!"

"This is Pung you're talking about!" said Jean "Our little brother, Pung, who's never let us down!" She spoke with the sharp voice of reason. Pung, Wayan and Ketut began to sing somewhere ahead of us, further down the trail.

"Jean!" called Pung. "We're waiting for you!"

"Just a minute!" Jean shouted, then said to me, "Remember our conversation about trust? They haven't betrayed us. They just want us to be happy and think we'll be happier when they say two hours than when they say five." I wrote this piece of logic in big white letters across the blackboard of my imagination.

In the gardens below the forest Pung, Wayan and Ketut began picking young fern shoots to cook up for dinner. While I was thinking about how hungry I was, they were doing something about finding us some food. When we passed the complex of temples above the road-head, our little band looked very shabby beside the finery of the folk preparing for a temple ceremony. In another few minutes we were again in the village where Rudy had dropped us the previous afternoon. The descent had taken just over five hours.

After piled plates of *nasi campur* at a roadside stall, we hitched a ride back to Pung's village. We made a brief stop at his family home to unload our bags and accept the mandatory cup of sweet coffee or tea, and then set out again for a much needed bath. About ten minutes north of the village there was a chattering brook that wound its way through a steep gorge among rice terraces and coconut palms. Pung led us down toward a stream-side shrine beneath an old, gnarled frangipani tree.

"My hot springs," he said.

The bathing place was a broad, shallow rock pool cut into the hillside above the level of the stream and surrounded by a thin hedge of hibiscus. Over this reached the frangipani, dropping its blossoms both onto the shrine and into the pool. The hot water came out of the ground a few yards up-slope from the tree and was channeled to three bamboo spouts at Balinese head-height. Most of the local population was still hard at work at home or in the fields, so we had the place to ourselves. The valley's rice fields had recently been harvested and flooded. The sound of running water was all about us. Above us, the mountain was wreathed once more in mist and mystery.

Sitting a polite distance uphill, we let Jean bathe first. Then Wayan and Ketut washed while Pung and I waited by the small shrine. By the time it was our turn we had been joined by one of Pung's second cousins. He spoke a little English and introduced himself as Madé while we undressed.

Pung was the first in. He dunked himself briefly under the hot water spout, yelped, and jumped in the river. "A bath should be cold!" he shouted. "Look at me!" He held out his arms for me to inspect. They were covered in goose-bumps.

"Strange, Pung. You're really strange," I said.

Madé seemed to have no such problem with the hot water, and I found the water pleasantly warm. I took a piece of pumice from a nook in the rock and began working on the Batukau grime that had blackened my feet. After a while I became aware that Madé was staring at me.

"What's up Madé?" I said. He was looking right at my genitals.

"Yours is a little larger than mine, but..." Cupped in his right palm, he placed himself into the stream of water. "...when I do this, mine gets bigger." Not a handsome creature at the best of times, his face was suddenly plastered with a smile that made him look something like a homicidal Cheshire Cat.

"Itches! Itches! Itches!" he intoned. I completed my bath with Pung in the stream. While Madé was busy washing, Pung nodded his way. He put his forefinger at an angle against his forehead as if it were the hour-hand of a clock. This meant Madé was "one o'clock." Pung grimaced and shook his head. Idiomatically, such a deviation from the "midday" norm was the equivalent of being "a brick short of a load."

On our way back to the village, an old man stopped us to pass the time of day. "Where have you been?" he asked.

"We just came down from the top of Mount Batukau," I said.

"How long were you up there?"

"One night. We went up there late yesterday."

"What did you go there for?"

"It's very beautiful. We wanted to see the view in the early morning."

The old man shook his head. This was obviously disturbing news. "The mountain is a very powerful god. You only go up there if you need some special help. If you want to see a beautiful view you can do that anywhere in Bali. That mountain is special."

The gate into Pung's family compound is half fallen down. The stairs up to it are deeply worn by the passage of family members, past and present. The wall across the front of the property serves its symbolic purpose, defining the space as a human habitation to all passing ghosts and spirits, but is otherwise in disrepair. The entire effect speaks of a household bulging at the seams where money that other families might use for maintenance is used to put rice on tables.

Immediately inside the gate was Pung's family's Eastern Pavilion, and to the north of that the family temple. Along the south wall stood a row of five *lumbungs*. These arch-roofed rice storerooms are where sheaves of Balinese rice are kept prior to pounding and cooking. The rest of the compound was a hodge-podge of low, two- or three-room buildings and kitchens. It wasn't immediately obvious that the orientation was the same as at Darta's house. The nine kitchens, four Northern Pavilions, three Western Pavilions, and two Eastern Pavilions were confusing, until you realized there were two households, side by side, within the same compound wall.

"How many people live here?" I asked Pung.

"My brothers and uncles live in the front half of the compound. My cousins live in the back. There are nine families and nine kitchens. Two families share some of the pavilions," he explained. "I'm not sure. I think there are about forty people."

Received as guests on Pung's father's Eastern Pavilion, we were served a dinner of boiled rice, fried soybean cake, green beans in grated coconut and marinated ferns: simple, delicious and satisfying. Our smiles of gratitude toward Wayan's mother, who had cooked, were heartfelt and all we could muster. Even the strong, sweet coffee did nothing to ease the weight of my eyelids or the nodding of my head. We excused ourselves and were shown to what I knew to be Wayan's room. "No, no, no," we protested. "Don't give us your room! Where will you sleep?" But he was an insistent host and we were too tired to fight. When Wayan left we flopped onto the single bed and were soon sound asleep.

"Damn that coffee!" I thought about two hours later. "Can't you wait 'til morning?" I asked my bladder. The answer was a definite, unequivocal, no.

I managed to get out of bed, pull on my pants, cross the room and get out of the door without waking Jean. I decided to head for the back of the compound and the woods beyond the back wall.

Walking around the end of the pavilion, I passed between Pung's brother's room and his kitchen, and nearly tripped over Pung's sister-in-law as she sat on her front step.

"Where are you going?" she said.

"I want a cat," I replied.

"A cat?"

"No, I mean a piss." The words are very similar in Indonesian. I was always confusing them.

"Over there, behind the *lumbung*," she said.

I waddled off into the shadows behind the nearest storehouse, unzipped my fly and waited for the flood. Behind me I heard the news of my adventure traveling like wildfire around the compound.

"Where's the guest going?" said a man's voice from the north.

"He's taking a piss," said the sister-in-law.

"A what?" said a woman in the center.

"A piss!" said the man from the north.

"What's all this noise then," said a another young man's voice from the west.

"The guest's taking a piss," chorused the other three.

"Where?"

"I sent him off behind the *lumbung*," said the sister-in-law.

"Good," said Pung's father. "He'd never have found his way down to the river."

"What's all this about piss in the *lumbung*?" said an old woman's sleepy voice.

Struck down with stage fright, my bladder refused to perform. I pressed on my abdomen, shook myself, jumped up and down. The earth in front of me remained stubbornly dry. Giving up, I waited an appropriate length of time before walking back. Half the people of the compound were sitting on their porches in their underwear, nodding and smiling to me as I passed.

"*Bagus*! Well done!" said Wayan's mother from across the corridor as I closed the bedroom door behind me.

I waited another two excruciating hours for everyone to go back to bed before heading out for the *lumbung* again. All I had to deal with the second time were the attentions of the compound's two resident dogs. They sniffed around my feet as an exotic-looking genie of steam rose into the night before me.

Jean and I were woken early by the pre-dawn roosters. We were kept awake by a household already in full swing. There were voices and laughter from one of the kitchens plus all the noise attendant with a Balinese compound's full complement of cats, dogs, chickens and children. We dressed and stepped out into the early light. Pung was already up, squatting on the newly-swept earth in front of his sister-in-law's kitchen, sipping a cup of tea. With a simple flick of his eyebrows he asked us if we wanted a cup. With a shake of the head and a smile we both declined.

"We're going for a walk first," Jean said. "To see the sunrise. Do you want to come?"

"Why not?" said Pung, leaving his half-empty cup on the kitchen stoop and standing up.

We turned north at the foot of the front steps, walking out of the village. To our left stood the combined precincts of the village's temples to Brahma and Vishnu. On our right was Pung's family's garden. We climbed a six-foot earthen bank topped by a line of bushes and entered a wide meadow through a gap in the hedge. At the other end of the meadow the land fell away steeply to a river. This slope was planted with fruit trees.

"How far does your land stretch?" I asked.

"From here down to the river and up to the next ridge." He pointed beyond the orchard to a distant line of coconut palms. The palms lined a path forming the eastern border of his land, perhaps a half-mile away.

"You have always said this is your land," I said. "Is it really just yours? What about your brothers?"

"Technically it's mine," he said. "As the youngest boy of a Sudra caste family, I will inherit it from my father. But all my brothers grow their rice and make their living off this land, so I have a responsibility to them first of all."

"This is where the organic farm could be," said Jean. "What do you think, Pung?"

"Well," he said, "we do have fresh spring water coming onto

this land."

We went back down onto the trail and headed uphill, away from the village.

"He didn't say no," whispered Jean to me. "A little seed of an idea." She smiled.

The path climbed a long incline and sank between high banks topped with coconut trees. A clear vein of water fretted along beside the trail, indecisively switching from one side to the other. Where the land leveled out, the path set out boldly around the broad crown of the hill but maintained its close company with the stream. Together they skirted a wood.

"Almost sunrise," said Jean. The full light of day was already upon the tops of the coconut trees on the horizon to our right. "Just a few more minutes." There was an old and twisted frangipani tree by the path. The soil about its roots provided a nice angle on which to sit. We parked ourselves in a little row, facing east.

The fields between us and the river were much broader than on Pung's land. We were higher too, and looked down on the tops of the trees in the valley. Their close packed crowns moved as one in the light breeze. To our left, around the shoulder of the ridge, the terrace walls were gathered up into steep pleats of green grass and rich chocolate soil. Below us this pattern resolved into a tapestry of blues and greens that melted the distinctions between sky and earth. I marveled at the beauty. Barely anything within my field of view was without the touch of human hands, yet everything worked together in a harmony so intensely satisfying it brought tears to my eyes. The water, the distant laughter of ducks, the breeze, the first diamond-bright lance of sunlight across the new day all conspired with the footpath and the hoe marks on the terrace walls. Humanity moved through these acres, a lover tending to the earth's every need, touching her wherever she willed and receiving her bounties in return.

"Pung, is this really as beautiful as I think it is?"

"It is," he said. "But before I left here, I wouldn't have thought so. I remember that, as a child, I walked further each day, in any direction, exploring this country. I came home late with my stomach complaining and my bag full of the frogs and grasshoppers I had caught. My mother cooked them up and I ate them with rice or potatoes. I don't lie to you when I say those were the happiest days of my life. I didn't yet know what electricity was. I didn't know that I was poor and I didn't know that your world existed, so I was free to be the richest little boy on earth. I'm a city boy now, as you always joke, but my heart is still here in this village and these fields. I know too much to be that happy again, but I want my child to know this happiness, at least once."

The sadness that had been with me since the flight across Sumatra, but which the night on the mountain had erased, began to creep over me once more. Pung must have seen this in my face because he said, "Don't think about what the world's becoming." He stood up. "Just think about the good things of the world-that-is. If we think about the bad then we don't want to do anything. Better to think about the good things: family and friends, mornings like this." He picked three blooms from the frangipani tree, slipped one behind Jean's ear, one behind mine, and kept one for himself. "C'mon," he said. "My tea's getting cold."

He started off down the path singing a well-known children's song:

I'm happy here.
I'm happy there.
My heart is happy everywhere.

Jean and I fell into step behind our pied piper. We sang all the way home.

CHAPTER 16

A Little Bit One O'Clock

By the time we got back to the family compound, dawn's coolness was already giving way to the day's heat. Jean and I went to Wayan's room to change. Pung came in after us with the flashlight and the clothes that had been borrowed on the climb.

"I'm sorry they're not clean," he said, "but I wanted to return them before they got permanently borrowed." We thanked him for his thoughtfulness.

There wasn't much room for us all in the small room, and I found myself leaning against the wardrobe in the corner while Jean bent over to stuff the dirty clothes in a bag. "Pung, Jean, look at this," I said. On the wardrobe door was a mirror. In the corner of the mirror was a faded photograph of Jean and me at a large temple. It was the main Batukau temple at the foot of the mountain's southeastern slope, many miles from where we began our climb. It was taken during my first visit to Bali, during the temple's anniversary ceremony, which always begins the day after *Galungan*. We were in full temple dress, standing beside a large white sign. "How sweet that Wayan keeps this picture of us. Where did he get it?"

"You gave it to him," said Pung. "And it's not of you. It's of our grandfather. Look. There he is in the corner. It's the only picture Wayan has to remember him by." The old man was in the bottom right-hand corner of the frame. The composition excised his left arm and both his feet. He wasn't even looking at the camera.

"We should go there again," said Jean, "on our way back to Ubud. We can thank the mountain for keeping us safe."

"We should have gone there before we started climbing," I said. "If we'd read this sign again, I'm sure it would have helped." We all looked at the photograph more closely, reading the sign. It was written in both Indonesian and English:

Those who are not allowed to enter the temple are:
1. Ladies who are pregnant
2. Ladies whose children have not got the first teeth
3. Children whose first teeth not fallen out yet
4. Ladies during their period
5. Dvotees [sic] getting impure due to death
6. Mad Ladies/Gentlemen
7. Those not properly dressed

"Look at five, six and seven," I said. "We weren't properly dressed for such a climb. We were certainly mad to try it. And I think death was the fifth guy in the sleeping bag with us, the one with his knees in my back."

"William," said Pung emphatically. "We had enough clothes and nobody died. And a little bit crazy is OK. You get too serious. You need to be a little bit one o'clock. It'll do you good."

After a breakfast of coffee and fried bananas we talked with Pung's father, the village priest responsible for the temple to Brahma. Describing the main temple complex on Mount Batukau, he took a piece of paper and drew an intricate diagram of lines, squares, triangles, and diamonds. It looked more like a circuit board diagram than a map.

"There are many stories I could tell you about the mountain," he continued. "When the Dutch were first in Bali at the start of this century, they wanted the kings to fight amongst themselves. Panjisakti, the King of Buleleng in the north, made war on this region, Tabanan. He wanted to kill everyone here, but decided to destroy the area's most important temple, at Batukau, instead.

His father had a vision before Panjisakti left for battle and said, 'If it's cloudy, don't go down to destroy the temple.' But Panjisakti wished for clouds, thinking they would cover his attack. When he arrived at the temple, the god of the mountain sent down a thick mist full of snakes and tigers and many other animals. Panjisakti and his entire army were killed."

"A dangerous mountain," added Pung.

"Now you tell us," I said.

"Amazing how quickly history becomes myth," whispered Jean.

Pung's father excused himself then and went out to tend to the goats in the garden. We went with Pung to the house of his eighty-five year old great-uncle. The old man was the local *dalang*, or shadow puppeteer. Pung called him *Pekak*, which is Balinese for grandfather. He called his great-aunt *Mbah*, or grandmother. When we arrived Pekak was up on his roof, fixing loose tiles.

"Ay, Jean! Come and visit! Come and visit!"

"You're busy. We'll come back later."

"Na. This is done. I'm coming straight down." He left a big hole in his roof and scuttled down a bamboo ladder to arrive at our feet. "Welcome! Welcome!" He flung his wiry arms around Jean, a rare public display of affection from a Balinese man to a woman. Then he gave me a hug, too. "It's been too long. Come and have a cup of tea or something. Sit down, you must be tired."

We sat down on a mat on his porch and exchanged news of families. Pung asked where Mbah was. She was next door making offerings. Pekak then asked me when I was going to come and study with him, as he always did when I visited. We asked how his grandson Ketut was, as we always did when we visited.

"Oh, he's off in Lombok working with the tourists still." Ketut is the family member Pekak wishes to train as the next *dalang*. "Nobody wants to learn this art anymore," said Pekak wistfully. "So I have to take my students where I can!" He grabbed me roughly by the wrist and glared up at me. "Even when they don't speak the language!" His expression cracked open and a peal of laughter poured forth. "When did you say you were coming to study with me?"

I must admit that the idea tickled my fancy. But not enough for me to commit to a serious study of the complete Balinese language, plus Sanskrit and the old Javanese tongue of Kawi, plus the Mahabharata and Ramayana epics and a number of indigenous tales. Training in the ability to give a different voice to at least fifty characters is also required, plus skill in playing the music, not to mention knowledge of all the offerings and ceremony surrounding a shadow puppet performance.

"Just give me a month of your time!" said Pekak. "Even a week would do, for a start."

We always went through this ritual. I always answered his protestations with, "Soon," or "Very soon," or "Maybe next time I'm here." We both fancied that he would eventually get his way. So he remained insistent but patient, just as he was with Ketut, fueling the spark of interest he knew to be in both our hearts.

"You'll come and watch me this afternoon, won't you?"

"Where are you performing?" Jean asked.

"Penebel. There's a cremation there today."

"If we're going to join him, I need to eat again first," I said to Jean.

"Go on then," said Pekak. "Go and eat. But be back here at two. That's when the bus leaves." The bus? Jean and I were impressed.

Back at Pung's house, lunch was ready and waiting for us. "I don't know why," I said to Pung, "maybe I've gotten used to being in Asia, but the day isn't complete anymore without some rice in my stomach." I caught the way Wayan's mother looked at me. It was the same way she would have looked had I said, "The day isn't complete without the sun rising and setting." While I was expressing the degree of my cultural adjustment, she could not conceive of life being any other way. That most Westerners would prefer to eat potatoes over rice would have sent her head spinning. Only a series of failed harvests or financial ruin would leave a modern Balinese without rice to eat.

We arrived back at Pekak's house at two o'clock sharp, just in time for another cup of sweet coffee, a selection of bananas, and an hour-and-a-half wait. Pekak was busy preparing himself and the tools of his trade. Pung, Jean and I got to talking about the bananas.

"...so this is a wood banana?" asked Jean.

"No," said Pung. "All wood bananas come from Tegalalang, the village where they carve all the wooden fruit that the tourists buy. This banana's from just down the street."

"So what kind of banana is this?"

"It's a wood banana."

"Isn't that what I just said?"

"Oh, I thought you meant a banana made of wood! What do you think this one is?"

"A king banana?"

"Is it!? I can never tell which one of them is the king. If he is the king we should be speaking more formally in his presence."

"Pung!"

"It's a green banana."

"We can see its color, but what kind of banana is it?'

"Really. It's called a green banana."

"And this one. Is this a milk banana?"

"No. Monkey penis."

"No need to be rude! I just asked what kind of banana it was."

"I'm not being rude. That's the name of the banana!"

And so the conversation went on and on until the bus arrived.

To refer to a small Suzuki flat-bed as a bus is to refer to the trail into Pung's village as a road: both descriptions are in essence factual but only from a certain perspective. Pekak, his assistant, two musicians, two large xylophone-like instruments, and Pekak's box of puppets piled into the truck. Jean, Pung and I sat precariously on the tailgate. The ruts in the road were so deep and the axles so low that the combined weight pinned the Suzuki to the spot. The three of us got off and walked behind the little truck as it bounced, scraped and slid its way along the potted and rutted excuse for a lane until it met the asphalt road through the next village. Only then did we climb aboard.

When we reached the household holding the cremation, we found that the family had already laid out mats for the *dalang* and the musicians to sit on in the middle of the family compound. The horizontal banana stem that would form the stage for the puppet theater was in place and framed by a pair of branches from a *dapdap* tree. Red, white and black threads had been tied between the branches to represent Brahma, Vishnu and Shiva. Being a daytime performance, there was no coconut oil lamp or white cloth screen with which to make the shadows.

The cremation proper was already complete. The shadow puppet theater was to be just one part of the cycle of ceremonies leading to the second, smaller and symbolic cremation.

"Pung," said Jean. "Did Pekak do this for your mother's cremation?"

"Of course!" said Pung.

"Where was I?"

"You were there. But you were already very tired."

The formalities of greeting the *dalang* were kept to a minimum. It was the presence of two foreigners that drew everyone's attention. A small multigenerational crowd plied us with questions.

"Oh! You're married." This really got them all interested.

"Do you have children?" pressed one of the women.

"Not yet," said Jean.

"No children!" The little gathering buzzed with the shock of the news.

"How long have you been married?" said a man from the back.

"Just over a year," I said, suddenly aware that I should have lied and said we were newly-weds.

"A whole year!" said the woman. The group started chattering to itself in Balinese. "Who's got the problem then?" she said to me, point blank. "You, or her?"

Coffee, cakes and cigarettes were served while the priests from the three village temples were called to the house. They would perform purification offerings while Pekak performed the puppet theater. Pekak only sipped at his coffee before excusing himself by asking to see the offerings that had been prepared specifically for him to use. Arranging everything took a further twenty minutes.

Once the village priests were busy with their ritual, the play was ready to begin. Pekak sat behind the banana stem and a tray of offerings. His assistant and his box of puppets were to his left. One metallophone was next to the box and the other was to his right. A musical prelude accompanied the prayers he conducted over the offerings and the box of puppets. When all was ready, he opened the box.

For the next few minutes the *dalang* and his assistant sorted through the puppets. Each was made from a sheet of leather and stiffened by a thin buffalo-bone spine that also formed the handle. Each was carved through with the intricate, lacy pattern that would define its shadow form in the nighttime performance. Many were brightly painted for the daylight theater. Those that Pekak needed were stuck by their handles into the banana stem. Some of these were tall and fine-featured princes and princesses. There were a couple of gods, a high priest and a dog. Most were jointed at shoulder and elbow to animate conversation. Pung told me that there would be no clear delineation between the right and left, the virtuous and the viceful, that characterizes the nighttime theater. "There won't be any fighting either," he said. "So we won't see 'Kak's teeth this afternoon." The *dalang's* false teeth often flew out in the heat of battle.

"Why is the daytime performance so much quieter?" I asked Pung.

"This isn't for us," he pointed out. "It's for the gods, to ensure the success of today's ceremonies."

Pekak's narration was barely audible. He seldom withdrew any puppets from the banana stem and only moved their hands to signify which character was speaking.

"What's the story?" asked Jean.

"It goes like this," said Pung. "At the very end of the Mahabharata, Yudhistira is the only one of the five heroes still alive. He and his dog climb the world's biggest mountain and are met at the edge of heaven by its ruler, Indra. Indra welcomes Yudhistira but says his dog can't come in. But the dog has come so far with Yudhistira and Yudhistira has promised his loyalty to the dog in return. So Yudhistira says he won't enter heaven. Then the dog turns into Dharma, the god of truth, and says that Yudhistira has passed his test. Yudhistira then enters heaven, but none of his family and friends are there. He demands to see his family, and is led to hell where he hears the cries of all the good people he has ever known. He has made a vow of loyalty to them too, and sits down to spend the rest of time with them. Then his test is really over and hell becomes heaven, and everyone lives happily together. And that's the end."

"Is there a moral to the story?" I asked.

"Of course! Yudhistira was always pure but once lied to his teacher, so he had to pay for that with a visit to hell. We see what heaven and hell are like, and we see that everything we do comes back to us eventually—even the smallest things. But it's not just about the after-life, because Yudhistira isn't dead. He has to follow his own sense of truth because even heaven and hell can be confused with each other."

The performance lasted just over an hour and concluded, without much fanfare, with all the puppets being put away in the reverse order from which they had been taken out. The audience was small throughout and consisted mostly of elders. Even they seemed to lose interest once they became aware of the chosen story. Without battle scenes and the much-anticipated moments when Pekak's false teeth fly out, the village children barely gave the event a second glance.

It was already well after dark by the time we arrived at the end of the asphalt and the beginning of the unpaved track into Pung's village. Once again, Jean, Pung and I walked behind the truck. It was another clear and starry night. The mountain was a silhouette off to our left. As we walked, I thought a lot about Yudhistira and his mountain, and Jean and I and our mountain, and all that had happened since we arrived in Indonesia. The ascent of Batukau felt like only the end of a climb that had begun all the way back in western Java. On the way up, there had been many joys and many obstacles.

I thought about the changes Pung had already experienced in his short life and how much less cluttered his mind seemed than my own; I thought of Yudhistira, and how his ultimate peace was born of his devotion to family, community and his personal truth. I was not about to go through the long ceremony to become a Balinese Hindu. I wasn't even sure if my way of seeing things bore any real resemblance to the Balinese world view. Rather, I realized that something of their way had infused my spirit in a manner that would lead me onward.

The truck stopped outside Pekak's front gate and we helped

unload the instruments and the box of puppets. The musicians and Pekak's assistant then bade us good-night and jumped back in the truck, hitching rides to homes at the other end of the village. Pekak invited us in. His wife had prepared us dinner.

"Sit with us, Mbah," Pung said to his great-aunt.

"No, no, no. I've already eaten. Eat. Tell the guests to eat until they are full," she implored. Although often the subject of polite conversation over cups of coffee with Pekak, the old woman seldom chose to show her face to Jean or me. It seemed she was embarrassed by her inability to speak Indonesian.

After the plates had been cleared we told Pekak about our adventures in Java. He was very interested in what we had to say about the temple on Mount Semeru and said he hoped to go there himself one day. When I looked at my watch and realized it was already after eleven, we thanked Pekak and Mbah for their generous hospitality and excused ourselves. Outside, on the street, we had a clear moonlit view across the rice fields up to the western mountains. The moon was bright and everything was bathed in silver light. Jean and I stood there, rooted in the peace and quiet of the moment. Pung came up beside me and put his arm around my shoulders.

"That's a big mountain," I said, nodding towards Batukau, "and that was quite a climb."

Pung shook his head slightly and sucked on his teeth. "In Bali we believe that while you are climbing a mountain you must never say how difficult it is, and you must never ask how far it is to the top."

I nodded again, and chuckled.

"Are you still out there?" shouted Pekak in Balinese from the house.

"Ya. We're still here," replied Pung. "We're just standing here, looking at the mountain."

"Looking at the mountain?" said Pekak, incredulous. "Why? What's it doing?"

Epilogue

In the end, Nyoman and his crew took another three months to complete our house. The bathroom counter remained a sore point throughout. At the end of November, when the counter's thickness broke the eight-inch barrier, we resorted to employing a Denpasar tiler who suggested we use marble instead of ceramics and did the whole job, beautifully, for under seventy-five dollars.

The tiler, Nyoman and his crew all finished on the same day. The house was finally complete. But we didn't move in until the first of December, when elaborate ceremonies of purification and animation were performed. As the priest sat among the offerings, chanting and ringing his little bell, Darta explained that the local spirit life had to be told that this was now our home and that we were not to be disturbed. The animation ritual recognized the spirit of the building itself: it was no longer wood, thatch, glass, sand, and cement; it was to be regarded as a living being and fed offerings accordingly.

On our first morning after moving in, we joked with Suda over coffee about the difficulties of the building process. "We almost went crazy!" said Jean. Suda nodded slowly, muttered his sympathies, and breathed deeply. Jean recognized the parody. "I know," she said, "different in America."

In time, we came to realize with what grace the builders had suffered all our blusterings and how well they had received our near-constant requirement that they "Do it again!" The scarred walls now remind us that electricity is both an overlay on the natural order of things and a new-fangled addendum to the Balinese concept of what a wall should be. The garden defied our fears and resurrected itself.

In the four years since the house was finished we have developed a small tour business. Darta and Pung are our partners, and the whole family is involved one way or another. We do three or four groups a year, exploring the Balinese culture. Work doesn't take up too much of our time. We spend a couple of days each week studying the island's culture and language, and I devote what time I can to my writing.

After the main roads of Ubud were widened, all were replanted with broad-leaved *rijasa* saplings. Many are thriving. In a few years we should be able to walk from our house to Darta's in shade once more.

Pung and Wetni's daughter, Hane, was born soon after the house was finished. At first they lived with Suda and Kadek, but after Suda's brother Putu returned from Flores with his family, the house was full to overflowing. Pung and Wet now live in a rented room a little way out of Ubud. Pung is a devoted father and brings Hane to play at our house while Wetni is at work.

Suda and Kadek had a third baby in 1996, a boy they are calling Komang. His arrival had a significant effect on his brother Adé, who is noticeably less destructive than he was. He always says hello now when we meet, and I find that I actually like him!

Suti, Darta and everyone at the family home continue to prosper. We visit frequently and Darta comes over to our house for a breakfast of bread and jam at least twice a week. He usually wears pants and a shirt nowadays, but his stomach still hangs out, and his coffee still goes cold while he gets carried away with some tall tale or other.

Postscript to the Second Edition

We are entering our ninth year in Bali. Our connection with the family continues to deepen, the house remains a beautiful place to live, and the tour business has a niche catering to yoga groups.

The biggest recent change at the family house came when Darta knocked down the decrepit Western Pavilion in late 2000 and set about replacing it with a structure that is three stories high from within the compound but only two stories tall from the lower street level. During construction he had to endure many comparisons to the title of this book, but rose above it all to create a beautiful, if unconventional space.

Jean and I are no longer as idle as we must have been when I wrote the epilogue. In 1997 we began exploring the islands beyond Bali, suddenly aware of how far we could travel speaking Indonesian. Roaming the archipelago we found we could gauge the vitality of traditional cultures by the ritual use of indigenous textiles. We also saw cultures degrading as families sold heirloom textiles to pay bills and weavers abandoned time-consuming traditions in favor of faster production. In response we created Threads of Life, an organization that commissions traditional textiles directly from weavers and encourages weavers to maintain the ancestral wisdom inherent in their art. Pung, Lolet and Weti are our partners in Threads of Life and we recently opened a gallery and educational space in Darta's new building, under the restaurant where Suti now sells her delicious home-cooked food.

To read recent news of the family visit www.RumahRoda.com. To see what Jean and I are doing go to www.ThreadsOfLife.com, or come and visit us all in Ubud at Rumah Roda, Jalan Kajeng #24.

Acknowledgments

First and foremost, I wish to thank the people portrayed in this book for sharing their life stories. I especially thank I Wayan Sudarta, I Madé Maduarta and I Nyoman Suda Riasta for opening their homes and their hearts to me. I am grateful for their constant friendship and the patience they have shown in guiding my exploration of their culture since 1989.

Among those who supported me in the writing of this book, a number stand out for special recognition. I owe the deepest debt of gratitude to my wife, Jean. She believed in this project from the start and has always been its loudest cheerleader. I wish to thank James Owen Mathews for guiding me through the creative process, and for inspiring me with his music. I especially thank Diana Darling for correcting numerous grammatical and cultural errors, Diana Hume for giving the manuscript direction and purpose, and Sue Winski, who brought consistency to the final draft.

I am grateful to Steve Epstein for proving to me that self-publishing could be both fun and rewarding. Without the assistance of Shirley Tanudjaja and I Dewa Ketut Ruditha Widya Putra, the production of this book would not have been possible.

My first readers were also very important. Their comments on the developing manuscript were invaluable. My thanks go to Jennie Arndt, Peter Damm, Ginny Howe, Lyn Howe, Hans Iluk, Rob Ingram, Virginia Jouris, Masaru Kawase, Hatsuyo Kitta, Donna Lambert, and Susan Tereba.

Back Row: Arep, Lolet, Ketut, Darta, Rudy, Putu, Suda, Abut, Pung, Malik. Middle Row: Ayun, Rida, Tutut, Lasmini, Sophan, Ibu, Turia, Suti, Hane, Kadek, Komang. Front Row: Kenyer, Shanti, Adé, Bayu

photo by Bryan Jones, 1997

photo taken in 1996

Darta

Suti

photo taken in 1988

Suda

Kadek

Ibu

photo taken in 1981

Roda

photo taken in 1993

Rudy

Adé

photo taken in 1993

Pung

photo taken in 1993

Wetni

Paman